I0629382

Improving Schools for Latinos

Creating Better Learning Environments

Leonard A. Valverde

Rowman & Littlefield Education
Lanham, Maryland • Toronto • Oxford
2006

Published in the United States of America
by Rowman & Littlefield Education
A Division of Rowman & Littlefield Publishers, Inc.
A wholly owned subsidary of The Rowman & Littlefield Publishing Group, Inc.
4501 Forbes Boulevard, Suite 200, Lanham, Maryland 20706
www.rowmaneducation.com

PO Box 317
Oxford
OX2 9RU, UK

Copyright © 2006 by Leonard A. Valverde

All rights reserved. No part of this publication may be reproduced,
stored in a retrieval system, or transmitted in any form or by any
means, electronic, mechanical, photocopying, recording, or otherwise,
without the prior permission of the publisher.

British Library Cataloguing in Publication Information Available

Library of Congress Cataloging-in-Publication Data

Valverde, Leonard A.
  Improving schools for Latinos : creating better learning environments /
Leonard A. Valverde.
       p. cm.
  Includes bibliographical references and index.
  ISBN-13: 978-1-57886-489-8 (hardcover : alk. paper)
  ISBN-10: 1-57886-489-5 (hardcover : alk. paper)
  ISBN-13: 978-1-57886-490-4 (pbk. : alk. paper)
  ISBN-10: 1-57886-490-9 (pbk. : alk. paper)
  1. Hispanic Americans—Education. 2. Latin Americans—Education—United
States. I. Title.
  LC2670.3.V35 2006
  371.829'68073—dc22   2006006470

♾™ The paper used in this publication meets the minimum requirements of
American National Standard for Information Sciences—Permanence of
Paper for Printed Library Materials, ANSI/NISO Z39.48-1992.
Manufactured in the United States of America.

To the many valiant individuals
I have known who championed and
worked to bring about meaningful public education
for Latino youth, particularly
Sal Castro, Joe Conway, Ray Ceniceros, and
Rosie Castro Feinberg,
and to the good persons truly devoted
throughout a full career to teaching
Mexican American students, especially
Roger Burke and Guy Sterner.

Contents

Foreword

The history of Latinos within American society has been one of inability to speak up or to speak out on issues that are of concern to them. Specifically, their exclusion from the institutional life of American society has kept them from being heard, even when their voices have been loud and their concerns compelling. Thus, denied access, they have had to experience in silence the denial, distortion, and trivialization of their historical experience. Moreover, they were led into believing that the fault lay in themselves and not in the institutions that govern their lives.

Over the past four and one-half decades, their voices have begun to ring out. Access to social institutions, particularly educational institutions, has provided them with forums within which to offer alternative views and the training and research that makes possible the generation of evidence to support them.

Nowhere have Latinos felt the weight of responsibility more heavily than in education. This supposedly enlightened institution is seemingly also one of the more retrogressive. Education continues to blame the victim for its own shortcomings rather than adapt its methods and policies to the differing populations and changing circumstances with which it is constantly confronted.

Thus this publication is at the cutting edge of the study of Latinos in the new century. The author of the publication, Dr. Leonard A. Valverde, provides a comprehensive, insightful, and intelligent perspective. In the first part, Dr. Valverde addresses the history, conditions, and future direction of Latino education. In chapter 1 he focuses on the educational experience of youths of Mexican descent with the intent of establishing a need for comprehensive and significant change of the educational system. In chapter 2 he focuses on rethinking and redefining how schools serving Latino students should be designed by addressing how we must tailor schools to fit the Latino culture and the Latino American experience.

In the second part, Dr. Valverde addresses how one views the world and behaves in organizational roles and how the organization functions in achieving its mission. In chapter 3 he discusses what staff development training must address to develop fresh and positive ways of thinking, to help staff undertake their roles in more constructive and productive ways, and to create a school community of believers. In chapter 4 he concentrates on laying out a set of practical requirements, including continual staff development, incorporation and use of technology, and formation of partnerships. These new requirements will enable the enlarging of capacity and the creation of more flexibility.

In the third part, Dr. Valverde focuses on transformation at the elementary and secondary school levels and instruction and learning at the classroom level. In chapter 5 he utilizes a "hothouse" perspective to address growing, nurturing, and enriching the whole child/family/community. He addresses the expansion of the school scope to include services to other critical players from the community. In chapter 6 he brings into sharper focus the continuing disconnect between the traditional Mexican culture and the school classroom. He addresses how to reorganize schools that continue to be overly regulated, exclusionary of low-income parents, and organized for individual competition while isolated for a greater part of the day.

In the fourth part, Dr. Valverde addresses evaluation, governance, and leadership. In chapter 7 he outlines how formative evaluation can be used as a tool to reinvent schools for collecting useful information and facilitating strategic planning. In chapter 8 he expands the scope of rethinking how schools should be constituted and elevates the reinvention of schools to a higher level by focusing on creating equitable relationships and reaching out to traditionally disenfranchised groups by listening to their concerns, ideas, and suggestions and building trust by acting on presented concerns.

In the fifth part, Dr. Valverde focuses on moving on to the next stage, whatever that stage may be. Chapter 9 provides individuals at different stages means to connect with each other and to learn from each other.

Thus, he provides a bridge that leads one to the next stage in the journey. In this chapter two objectives are accomplished: (1) connecting works in progress to help create stronger and better schools and (2) helping practitioners in efforts to advance the transformation of schools by identifying links to resources and technical assistance.

In summary, Dr. Valverde has, in this publication, taken steps to begin to bring the new Mexican American school into focus by providing a variety of valuable information as he emphasizes (1) redefinition of schools, (2) community-centered institutions, (3) culturally asset-based schools, (4) real parent participation, (5) a variety of programs, and (6) partnerships with various agencies. Thus, it appears that he is making a significant contribution to education in the 21st century. Teachers need this book, America deserves it, and our students will demand it. There is yet much work to be done. We need to capture the sustained attention of educational policy makers and influence their decisions and actions. Our voices are now loud, clear, and eloquent, but they are often unheard. We must press forward to bring influence to bear on the decision makers who determine the future of our educational experiences.

Reynaldo Contreras, San Francisco State University

Preface: The Time Is Ripe

I wanted to write this book about 30 years ago, when I first started my higher education professorship and after leaving public schools as a teacher, administrator, and instructional supervisor of math teachers. As I complete this writing, I realize I was not fully ready to do so then. Additionally, 30 years ago I would not have thought that we would still be facing the same problems and that the outcomes would continue to be the same—unacceptable. More important, for different and many reasons, 30 years ago the majority of the then leadership in public education was also not ready to create schools as defined and described herein. However, today I believe a window, and in some places a door, is open to creating significant change and at the magnitude necessary, although not at the systemic level. In short, K–12 public school leadership is ready and in many communities is already translating concepts into practice.

Over these 30-plus years, the demographics have shifted greatly such that Latinos are now the largest ethnic/racial subpopulation in the United States (42.7 million). We need to add to this 2005 Census Bureau count the undocumented Latino numbers, estimated at between 11 and 12 million. The undocumented count is important because of who it represents: Spanish speakers, who for the most part are unassimilated into a multicultural society. Also, Latinos are no longer a regional population, isolated to certain parts of the United States. Instead they are a national population, found in significant numbers in the New England states and on the east coast, historically in the midwest (particularly in Chicago and Detroit), and of course in large numbers in the southwest and on the west coast.

In the last decade of the 20th century, Latinos of Mexican ancestry have rapidly increased in such southern states as North Carolina and Georgia, in northwest states such as Oregon and Washington, as well as in Alaska and Hawaii. In many school districts across the country, particularly metropolitan centers (e.g., New York City, Miami, Chicago, San Antonio, Los Angeles, Dallas, and Houston), Latinos are the majority student body. Latinos of Mexican descent who are born in the United States are commonly referred to as Mexican Americans or Chicanos, and those born in Mexico who are recent arrivals are called Mexicans. These two basic groups account for 70% of the total Latino U.S. population.

Because Latinos of Mexican ancestry are the largest subgroup and are national in geographic scope, this book will have utility to a broader venue of educators and more communities across the country. In turn, by better educating this fast-growing Mexican ancestry population, the economic future of the United States as well as the world will be strengthened. Just one example of past and present economic prowess is the agricultural wealth in California due primarily to the Mexican field worker, or *bracero*. In a highly technological and information age society, the Latino population will need to be much better educated so they can help sustain the U.S. economic engine. Also, local communities will be better served by developing Latinos for future civic leadership, as is the case now in Los Angeles, Miami, San Antonio, and Denver with Latino mayors and in the state of New Mexico with a governor.

Beyond the demographic increases and beyond becoming a national population that will provide potential future benefits to the nation, there have been significant allowances that permit schools to provide better instructional programs. The educational progress for students of color began with and as a result of the civil rights movement. The educational development began with the famous 1954 U.S. Supreme Court ruling to desegregate schools (*Brown v. Topeka Schools, Kansas*); continued with the passage in 1963 by the federal government of the Elementary and Secondary Education Act (ESEA), Title I legislation; followed by Title VII, the Bilingual Education Act; the 1974 *Lau* Guidelines; the promotion of multicultural education in the 1980s; the emphasis on closing the achievement gap between whites and minority students; the focus on dropout prevention; and the decade of the 1990s with the accountability movement, bringing national school reform into existence. With the start of a new millennium, an added phase has begun with the federal government's No Child Left Behind Act, a much-needed positive mental construct for teaching all children of color.

Given these educational movements from the 1960s to the present, researchers, practitioners, and others have studied, examined, and evaluated pilot projects and federally funded initiatives. Also, private foundations have supported model intervention programs and required assessment of these efforts. Equally, federal and private funds have supported the preparation and development of change agent leaders. As a result of all these reports, documentation, and analyses (as well as leadership training), scholars, educators, and policy makers have learned many lessons. Hence the time is ripe for practitioners to create schools for the Latino population that has inhabited the United States the longest and schools that will consistently produce student learning and community development through new paradigms. Also through the federal government's push for school accountability, taken up by state legislatures, there is a pressing need for school reform. While we cannot discuss all the aspects of things learned (e.g., new philosophy, new pedagogy, new curricula, new models, new practices), this book will provide a fundamentally sound blueprint—a grand architectural design that many practitioners are seeking to put into place. I am sure experienced practitioners will recognize many parts of the comprehensive effort, but through this book they now will be able to see the whole picture and understand that each component is interlocked, perhaps explaining why a certain component may not have worked as well as it should have. That is, some necessary pieces were not in place to produce the expected outcome.

Improving Schools for Latinos provides the reader with a variety of valuable information by way of the following: (1) conceptual frameworks to think or rethink about how to lead and direct schools, (2) guidelines for how and why instruction and learning should be organized to improve teaching and increase student achievement, (3) practical ideas about how to establish a positive learning community, not just to promote student learning but also to have schools become service centers that will assist (Spanish-speaking) parents and others, and (4) identification of programs already in place that work to increase achievement and strong student self-concept.

In short, this book emphasizes ideas that should be in place if Mexican American students are to achieve scholastically:

- Redefinition of schools
- Community-centered institutions
- Culturally asset-based schools, where home language is a must!
- Real parental participation, not just school-prescribed ways
- Variety of programs (ESL, bilingual, dual language, multicultural) for different generations and socioeconomic status (SES) Latinos
- Partnerships with various agencies
- Interlocking and connectedness of schools, from preschool to graduate school

Because of all the demands by various sectors (federal and state governments, businesses, parents, community advocacy groups) and the lessons educators have learned, the time is ripe to create community schools for Latinos of Mexican descent—schools that will yield better educated Mexican Americans by serving their neighborhoods fully and in so doing strengthen the total community and the nation.

Acknowledgments

This book came to fruition as a result of good help from a few others. As always, books get into print when a publisher agrees to produce the manuscript. To convince a publisher there is a market is no easy task. However, I have been fortunate to have a lasting and long relationship with Mitch Allen. While we were both visiting Chicago for AERA, in conversation with him I shared my problems with a certain publisher in getting them to accept my prospectus as is. It was Mitch who suggested I try Scarecrow Press (later turned into an affiliate of Rowman and Littlefield publishers), and he followed up with an email to Tom Koener, the publisher. As they say, the rest is history. Without Mitch's friendship and help and Tom's patience, this book would have remained in my head and not in the hands of the readers.

Second, with much fondness and great appreciation, I recognize my wife, Josie, of 40 years and even longer, my lifelong partner (since junior high days). She suspended her employment to work on the writing of the manuscript. She looked up citations, edited drafts, found new sources, provided alternative ideas, made contacts, and did much more. Clearly, without her help, I would not have been able to complete the manuscript within the extended deadline.

Third, I am extremely fortunate to have the services of Sandra Chavez-Lopez as my administrative associate. She not only worked on the manuscript preparation and presentation, such as formatting tables and developing lists, but also handled much of the HBLI workload, relieving me of my typical work press and thus allowing me to concentrate my time on the writing of this book.

Fourth, I thank the Civil Rights Project at Harvard University, which facilitated a Visiting Senior Scholar appointment with the Graduate School of Education during the fall semester of 2005. CRP provided me an office space and access to Harvard's extensive library and required very little of my time in return.

Last, there were a few persons who contributed direct help to some of the content of the book. One is Rey Contreras, a colleague "in arms" who graciously took time away from his heavy demands to write the foreword. Among the others was Rosie Castro Feinberg.

Part I

HISTORY, CURRENT CONDITIONS, AND FUTURE DIRECTIONS

Chapter 1 begins by reporting the historically (and unfortunately) negative education experience of Latino students of Mexican descent, no matter their status or generation (new arrivals born in Mexico or born in the United States and either first generation or other) in public schools. The intent here is not to blame past educators or place a guilt mind-set on current educators but to establish a strong case for comprehensive and significant change. Systemic change is called for when we examine the school indicators that measure success. The most common are low annual test scores on standardized instruments, the long-standing achievement gap between white students and brown students, the persistent high dropout rates, and the disproportionate overrepresentation of Chicano[1] students in remedial and special education classes. Along with this discussion, the chapter identifies some of the likely causes leading to these banal outcomes, such as educators having little familiarity with Latino students; minimal inclusion of the Latino culture in schools, particularly in curricula; typifying Hispanic communities as being poverty stricken and all that is associated with poverty; negatively biased and stereotypic thinking about students and parents of color; a high reliance on rules, producing a restrictive climate; and a rigid tracking system, resulting in sorting into skilled labor curriculum and not college-bound classes. All these conditions and actions have created a commonly held attitude that blames the victim and the parents (i.e., the schools cannot succeed with these students until and unless the students and their parents change).

The chapter continues by addressing some of the recent trends that set the stage for taking a much-needed new direction in the education of

Latino students of Mexican descent. Among the positive trends are the successful legal challenges to state school funding formulas, bringing more financial equity into play; the development of bilingual education and the start of dual-language programs; and the promotion of multiculturalism and the capitalization of a mother tongue as an asset. Some of the setback trends identified are the antibilingual western-state referendums that take away from educators the option to use home language as a tool of instruction, as well as outgrowths of the accountability movement (e.g., raising standards and high-stakes testing and the stigmatizing of schools as underperforming and failing).

Chapter 2 makes the effort to rethink and redefine how schools for Latino students should be designed. If our past and present system of organizing schools has not been successful to the extent wanted by educators, parents, business leaders, and civic leaders, then we must tailor schools to fit the Latino culture and the Latino American experience. To undertake this major overhaul, the obligations and tasks are in many ways greater and more complex and yet in some ways simple. In order for schools to fulfill their educational responsibility in a more robust and effectual way, they will require more resources, reorganization, and linkages to other institutions in a more functional way.

Chapter 2 introduces how national, state, and local agencies can play a role; how business partnerships can be expanded; and how professional education associations can be more cooperative and less competitive. The chapter shares ideas about restructuring schools, broadening their mission, and increasing support from a greater variety of agencies.

NOTES

1. The term *Chicano* is used by some to refer to a Latino of Mexican ancestry born in the United States. The other typical descriptor is Mexican American.

Chapter One

Why We Must Start Now to Create New Schools for Mexican Latinos

There are at least three main reasons why as a society we must create 21st-century schools to educate U.S. Latinos of Mexican origin. The three reasons are rooted in the past, the present, and the future. The historical reason is not so much to undo past wrongs as it is to discontinue unproductive practices. Regrettably the negative educational experience of Mexican Latinos started with the end of the U.S. war with Mexico in 1848. Even though Mexicans made a conscious choice to stay in homes they had built and in lands they had worked prior to the southwest becoming U.S. territories, and even though they were given rights and citizenship by the Treaty of Guadalupe Hidalgo, their educational treatment was not the same as other settlers moving westward. Even as the public educational system in the United States began to grow, develop, and become a basic fiber in the U.S. society's fabric as we know it today Mexican youths born as American citizens did not benefit from public education as did most white immigrants. This long-lasting shortcoming of public schools has been well documented over time by historians (see Tyack, 1974), along with the banal experience of Mexican Americans by agency reports (see U.S. Commission on Civil Rights, 1970–1976) and by educators (see Sanchez, 1946; Carter, 1970).

The second reason to create better schools is found in our country's ongoing obligation to its citizens. As a nation based upon the concept of democracy, such a philosophy and its governance system work well only if its citizenry is educated. So it is that each state is required to provide a free public education (grades K–12) to its residents. While clearly a public education has been and is in place across the country, access and effectiveness have been mixed and uneven to this day.

Besides trying to reverse the past wrongs and society's trying to fulfill its responsibility to all of its citizens and future workforce, there is a third compelling reason for creating a new positive educational experience for U.S. citizens and residents of Mexican ancestry. While the first two reasons focus on the moral imperative and the past, the third reason rests on the practical necessity of building a strong economic future for the nation. The United States has become more diverse because it continues to be a nation of immigrants, and these new waves of immigrants, primarily populations of color, must be educated. Since North America's economic development and democratic government will need to be sustained by this new majority,[1] the United States must educate its total population. As of 2005, Hispanic Americans have become officially the largest population of color (14.4%) in the United States, surpassing African Americans (12.8%).

PAST PRACTICES MUST CHANGE FASTER THAN THEY HAVE

The failure of public education for students of Mexican descent is not recounted herein to point fingers of blame. The intent here is to lay the basis for the need to redesign schools now. Even though it may appear the argument is moot, there appears to always be a call for reasons or justification why school officials need to move away from the outmoded past practices and environments. Since the intent of this book is to provide ideas of what should be created, space devoted to the negative will be restricted in order to have expanded space for later discussion of what needs to be done in schools to provide solid learning and community service. Hence, the most significant and revealing negative indices are shared in brief form. Also, likely factors that have produced unwanted results are shared, again for a constructive purpose, to lay the basis for what not to continue to do in the future. Hopefully, by sharing these factors, valuable time will not be wasted in arguing over the pros and cons of these past and current counterproductive policies. After reading this section, the reader should conclude that much of what has occurred in the past in schools with regard to Mexicans, Mexican Americans, or Chicanos was due mostly to societal dynamics. That is, public schools reflected the general and prevalent thinking and were the state's social agencies that carried out the legislative will of the time.

In the beginning (in our case after the year 1848) and throughout the remaining 19th century, public education in the west was to a great extent underdeveloped, with very few schools and even fewer formally prepared teachers. Mandatory school attendance was still not the law of the land. Under these conditions, a vast number of Mexican youths, made citizens through the 1848 Treaty of Guadalupe Hidalgo, were not in school. With the start of the 20th century, the educational experience of Mexican Americans was comparable to that of African Americans (i.e., inferior due to the law of the land at the time). The U.S. Supreme Court decision in the 1896 *Plessy v. Ferguson* case permitted "separate but equal" public facilities to exist and be legal. Even with the passage of mandatory attendance (1920s) and construction of schools in big cities, Mexican Americans in rural areas did not have access to schools. Those Mexican Latinos living in large cities had to go longer distances to get to "neighborhood" schools. When they did not attend regularly due to economic family hardship or other reasons, the mandatory attendance rule was either not enforced or vigorously enforced, dependent upon what was best for the school. In both cases, the practice was detrimental for Mexican Americans. Also in place in this time period by state law was the prohibition of students to speak Spanish on school grounds. Students caught speaking Spanish in school even on the playground, during lunch or recess, were punished, typically by physical paddling. (It needs to be noted that even now there are isolated cases where this punishment practice for speaking Spanish on school grounds still exists; see Ryman & Madrid, 2004.)

Even when in 1954 the U.S. Supreme Court banned school segregation in the famous *Brown v. Topeka, Kansas* case, the educational experience and conditions did not change for Mexican Americans, as was the situation for African Americans. In fact, in the southwest, African Americans were "desegregated" with Mexican Americans, since Mexican Americans were considered white. It was not until 1970, in the *Cisneros v. Corpus Christi Independent School District* court case that Mexican Americans were considered for the first time an identifiable ethnic group other than white for school desegregation purposes. School busing, the first major strategy used to desegregate schools, did very little to upgrade school facilities and dismantle the inequality of school conditions for either Mexican Americans or African Americans, as well as other segregated groups.

National and state laws as well as other social conditions accumulated over 150 years produced entrenched negative outcomes. First and foremost, classroom subject-matter achievement by Mexican Americans was below par as measured by standardized tests. In fact, the longer a Mexican American stayed in school, the less achievement occurred (i.e., an inverse relationship existed for most Mexican American students). Stated another way, the higher the grade levels Chicanos advanced, the further behind in grade-level achievement they became. To illustrate this point, the 2005 National Assessment of Educational Progress (NAEP) report card shows that eighth-grade Hispanics scored 27 points lower than whites in math, and fourth-grade Hispanics scored 20 points lower. It is even worse when we compare English language learners (ELLs) with non-ELLs (see Table 1.1). Second, there exists an achievement gap between Mexican American students and white students. Even after closing this achievement gap became a national priority (during the 1980s), the achievement gap has widened or stayed the same.[2] Why? Using the same model to produce a different outcome is illogical. Third, a disproportionately large number or greater percentage of Mexican Americans were placed in remedial educational programs or placed into occupational tracks or special education programs with a label of retardation attached. Again, when studies revealed a statistically disproportionately high inclusion of Chicano and Mexican Latinos in special education, the numbers did not decrease.[3] Fourth, many Latinos of Mexican descent left school before the 12th grade. Thus, it is well documented that they have had the highest dropout rate of any other group of color.[4] In some schools where their enrollment is 90% or more, the dropout rate has been as high as 60 to 70%! The national average has been as high as 44% (Valverde, 2002). It naturally follows that high school graduation rates are the lowest. In a March 2002 U.S. Census Bureau report, only 26.7% of Latinos of Mexican origin were high school graduates. While the high school graduation numbers increased in the 1980s and 1990s, the numerical increase in graduation was due to general population increase. Percentages remained as low as before.

Numerous studies (Ramirez & Castaneda, 1974; Duran, 1983) examining the experience of Mexican Latinos in public schools in the southwest

Table 1.1.   2005 National Math and Reading Scores for Fourth and Eighth Graders

Students	Fourth Grade				Eighth Grade			
	Math	Difference[1]	Reading	Difference	Math	Difference	Reading	Difference
Whites	246		229		289		271	
Hispanics	226	−20	203	−26	262	−27[2]	246	−25
Non-ELLs[3]	240		222		281		264	
ELLs	216	−24	187	−35	244	−36	224	−40

Notes: 1. Difference is calculated by subtracting Hispanics' scores from white students' scores. This difference, or lower score, is the achievement gap. 2. Also note that the achievement gap is greater in the eighth grade than in the fourth grade in math and reading. The lone exception is in reading for Hispanics in eighth grade, down 1 point from 26 to 25. 3. ELLs stands for English language learners.
Source: National Assessment of Educational Progress, 2005.

have concluded that the aforementioned adverse outcomes are tied to the psychological framework produced in schools. In essence, the schools see students of color as immigrants coming from foreign countries. The public schools are charged with the responsibility to acculturate and assimilate these groups. Our country's perspective has been for persons to adopt the American identity, values, and customs, and in so doing these individuals abandon their homeland identity—in short, it is a concept of exchange, a substitution process, a program to transform persons. This acculturation process is not the mythical melting pot theory (i.e., components of an immigrant's culture are woven into the existing cultural milieu). The best way to see how this subtractive assimilation practice works on Mexican Americans is to describe how their language is treated in schools. Prior to the 1960s, non-English-speaking students were not only prohibited from using their home language but also put into a "sink or swim" language situation (i.e., they were put into an all-English classroom without any English as a second language [ESL] instruction).[5] The underlying premise in this approach is the more students are forced into hearing and using the English language, the faster they will learn it. However, this forced emergence and fast treatment has considerable learning detriments. First, the student is lost and in a stressful daily situation. This trying experience is comparable to the traumatic separation that five-year-olds face each year leaving the safe and known confines of home and mother when entering kindergarten. There is a high level of personal discomfort. Without a base of understanding, much confusion and doubt is created in the child's mind. Over time, the child develops feelings of insecurity and low self-concept about his or her learning ability. Second, there are many weeks and months of lost learning opportunities. Students cannot learn subject-matter content if they do not have command of the classroom instructional language.

But the school acculturation process has an even greater negative consequence on Latino students. The psychological reaction is most harmful. Through this addition/subtraction process, indirectly students come to believe their home language (subtraction) is not as good as English (addition). They are asked to erase their homeland customs, their celebrations, and worse, their value base, and in so doing they develop a sense of shame in their culture. As an example of how basic this exchange is, a food example is offered. Tortillas are to Mexican Latinos what bread is to most white Americans. Prior to the emergence of the multicultural education movement, sons and daughters sent to school with burritos or tacos in their lunch bags where ashamed to eat at school. They somehow knew they were supposed to eat sandwiches made with slices of white bread. Subconsciously, tortillas were not as good as bread. (Ironically, tortilla wraps are the current rage in chic restaurants and fast-food venues.) Extending this example to the broader context, to be Mexican was inferior to being American. In short, these children were asked to deny their family identities and transform themselves into Americans.

Mexican Latinos had three options with regard to the school's socialization process: conform (accept), resist (with adoption), or reject (drop out). If they conformed by giving up their family/ethnic identity or at least a great deal of it, they developed a low self-esteem about themselves and created an unnatural distance with their extended families. If they resisted, they were treated as troublesome (e.g., disciplined by the school), given lower grades (not necessarily earned), suspended from school due to repeated offenses of school rules, held back in grade level due to lack of cooperation and excessive absences, and so on. If they rejected the socialization process (i.e., they did not believe they had to give up their Mexican identity in order to be an American), they left school altogether, or dropped out. A precursor to leaving school (becoming a dropout) was not going to school (establishing a record of excessive absenteeism) or leaving school by midday (referred by students and teachers as "ditching"). Officially, they became school dropouts. However, these nonconformists would say they were forced out, or became pushouts.

This psychological construct is a fundamental tenet that will be revisited throughout the book. Closely associated with this socialization construct is the prevailing belief that Latinos of Mexican ancestry were culturally deprived or educationally disadvantaged; as such they we. ` seen as persons with deficiencies, and remedial educational programs were in order. In short, low expectation about this student population was the norm. This prevailing belief determined school treatment and justified student outcomes. After all, under this perception, the fault of low achievement, absenteeism, and ultimately high dropout rates was created by the students themselves, not the school policies. Parents of these kids were also seen as contributing to the problem. The general misperception held by teachers was that Mexican parents did not value education and therefore took no interest in having their children attend school. However, studies and school surveys show just the opposite.[6] These parents value education highly, they want their children to learn as much as possible, and they respect teachers greatly. However, because of their limited ability in the English language and their difficult economic situation, they are afraid to go to the school or do not have time to go to the school during school hours. In addition, school personnel have not tried to encourage and accommodate parents to be more active in their children's education.

THE FUTURE IS NOW

As we begin the third millennium, the one thematic constant in the United States is that change is inevitable. The other social constant is that certain national and historical trends continue. Caught between these two constants are schools. Additionally, in order to serve America's future needs, new 21st-century schools, made up of a growing diverse student population, will need to be redefined. Schools of the past have not served Latinos adequately. Given a different and more dynamic future, new schools will need to be designed. In addition, schools that will have Latinos (recent arrivals, first generation, low and middle income, Spanish or English speakers) as their major student body will need to substantively reconstitute themselves, since the United States will require a highly technologically skilled workforce and more civic leaders to serve multicultural communities. Both employees and societal builders will be coming from this high growth population.

Let us begin with the major changes that have occurred and those changes that have meaning for the future. One of the most obvious changes is that the United States is now a high-technology country. Communication and information accessibility is greater in capacity and faster in processing. Aided by technology, a knowledge explosion is occurring. This technology innovation has created another change, a global economy—an economy of global production (NAFTA), stock-market investment, and international corporations. A third change is greater mobility of residents due to employment relocation. Besides moving from one employer to another, persons are changing professions, more than once, in their career life spans. A fourth change is that urban society is becoming stratified, described by a two-by-two matrix of urban settings: major metropolitan centers and large cities both having an inner-city, low-income core surrounded by middle-class suburbia. In rural America, large mechanized farms and dairies support these complex urban societies. (Lately, these large farms have decreased in number.) Fifth, because of the first four changes, there is a necessary interdependence and closer connectedness. One sector directly or indirectly affects another sector and at times more than one sector. For example, the lack of food production in one country impacts the availability of food in the United States. Similarly, food prices are altered accordingly. Another simple example is overseas or off-shore factories. These "factories" determine supply and demand of the U.S. labor force as well as salary scale and pricing of items.

Now we turn to the historical and national trends that have continued over a long period of time. The United States was founded as a nation of immigrants. Associated with the immigration trend is the second defining character of the United States (i.e., it continues to be an experiment in democracy). As such, the United States strives to protect the rights of the individual and at the same time tries to strike a balance to uphold the will of the majority. Third, to the majority of the world masses, America continues to be seen as the land of opportunity. The Statue of Liberty symbolizes this perception of promise. The major steel girder that buttresses this world belief is the principle that persons who work hard, apply themselves, and demonstrate performance can and will achieve. Fourth, because the United States represents the land of freedom and opportunity, immigrants will continue to come, and the U.S. population will continue to grow in number and in diversity. The total U.S. population as of 2005 was estimated to be at 293.6 million. Of more significance than the continued growth in raw numbers is the changing face or multiple faces that make up these numbers.

Diversity in the U.S. population has increased due to immigration, birthrates, and interracial relationships. The last decade of the 20th century had the second highest immigration numbers; the largest numbers were during the 1890–1910 period. Whereas during this first period, the bulk of the immigrants came to the United States from middle and southern Europe, the most recent immigrant surge was from Asian countries and South America. The one constant during these twin immigration peaks has been the migration of Mexicans into the United States, both legally and illegally. As the population in Mexico has grown, so has its migration numbers into the United States. Fueling this migration has been the poor economic conditions in Mexico and the unskilled worker demands in the United States (e.g., produce growers needing crop pickers; domestics for hotels and resorts; low-skilled industries such as janitors and sanitation workers).

The 2000 Census count shows birthrates are greater for nonwhites and therefore family sizes are larger. The average family size for Latinos of Mexican origin was 4.1 compared with 3.1 for non-Hispanics (U.S. Census Bureau, 2002). Life spans are longer for nonwhites as well. These characteristics translate into the growth figures in the following way. Entering the 21st century, the greater percentage increase in the total population growth is due to groups of color. These trends are resulting in a major shift not seen before. The percentage of the total white population is decreasing, while the percentage of groups of color is increasing. This proportional shift is creating a new and different balance: Traditional white majority is now becoming the minority. For example, in California, the white population is no longer the majority. Combining the groups of color (Latinos, African Americans, Asians, Native Americans, and others) puts them in the majority. In high-growth states, such as California, New York, Texas, and Florida, the greatest increases are being made by groups of color. In Arizona, Nevada, California, and Texas, the greatest increase has been made by Hispanics. A good illustration is Arizona. At the turn of this century, its population increased from 3.6 million to 5.1 million. Of this 1990–2000 increase, Latinos of Mexican heritage grew from 688,338 to 1.3 million, or an 88% increase, the most of any subgroup in the state (Valverde, 2002).

In addition to the Latino population growing the fastest, it is also the youngest. While the percentage of whites under the age of 18 years is 24.4, for Latinos it is 34%. For Latinos of Mexican ancestry it is even higher at 37.1% (U.S. Census Bureau, 2002). Thus, we find a higher percentage of school-age Latinos than white school-age children. In 2005, the total enrollment of students in K–12 grades was at an all-time high of 42.5 million. Of this total, Latinos constituted 16.2%, or 6.8 million (Chronicle of Higher Education, 2001). The total Latino population was 13.8% of the total U.S. population. The Latino student population for the entire country is even higher at 17.8% (NCES, 2005). Percentages of Latino student enrollments within certain states are even higher. For example, in California Latinos make up 32.4%, in Texas they make up 32%, and in New Mexico they make up 45% of student enrollments.

Before leaving student enrollments, a particular Latino student enrollment component must be pointed out, those of limited-English-speaking ability. In a 10-year period (1986–1996), limited English proficient (LEP) student national enrollment increased from 1.5 million to 3.4 million, or more than doubled in number (IDRA, 2001). Also, a 1996 Harvard study reports that Latino students in large cities are more segregated now in public schools than before the 1954 *Brown* ruling (Orfield & Eaton, 1996).

The 2000 Census count allowed more persons to identify themselves as biracial (i.e., half white and half African American, half white and half Latino, half African American and half Asian, and so on). In addition, the official acknowledgment of this long-standing status within the United States—biracial individuals—cemented a new social attitude toward diversity, expressed openly at the end of the century. Diversity is now seen as an enriching quality. Understanding other cultures or speaking more than one language helps individuals function and compete in a global economy. Before this view, being biracial was seen as detrimental (e.g., "half-breed"). Because of this negative bias, some biracial persons, particularly those half white and half black, tried to pass as white and hide their black ancestry. A few strong-willed dual-racial persons were unwilling to deny one half of themselves and give up their bicultural identity in order to be classified as American. This new attitude toward diversity and identity is best illustrated by an interview with Tiger Woods. He was asked by a writer what seemed to be a routine question: how it felt to be pronounced the year's world's best golfer and what it meant for him, being that he is African American. The response was unexpected by the news media and white America. He replied that he was not African American, he was a combination of Asian and African American. For him to acknowledge only his father's race would be to indirectly deny his mother and to put less value on his Asian culture. This type of thinking was not acceptable to him and is now becoming the norm for many of his generation.

A CHANGING MEXICAN AMERICAN PROFILE

Just as the profile of the U.S. population is changing substantially, so too is the profile of Latinos of Mexican ancestry. This population in some ways remains the same and yet is different. Latinos of Mexican origin have always been heterogeneous, yet the public image has been painted wrongly as homogeneous. To provide an accurate heterogeneous picture, four components are described: (1) geography—where they live, (2) socioeconomic status—employment and consumption, (3) language usage, and (4) generation outlook.

Latinos were once perceived as local or regional populations, confined to a few states. The old view limited Latinos of Mexican descent to the southwestern states; Puerto Ricans to the northeast coast, primarily New York and New Jersey; and Cubans to the southeast, particularly south Florida. These old patterns were very limited and inaccurate. For example, this old regional view would constantly omit the large number of Latinos of Mexican ancestry who settled in the Great Lakes area early in the 20th century. Originally, migrant farm workers settled in Chicago and Detroit when they found better jobs in the auto factories. (In fact, it is little known that Chicago has the second largest concentration of Mexican Americans in the United States, Los Angeles having the first.) Also, the old regional view forgets the number of Mexican migrant workers who followed the harvests to the northwestern states of Washington and Oregon and who settled there as well.

More important, Latinos of Mexican ancestry are now spreading out in large numbers to other regions of the country, particularly into traditionally southern states. Census numbers for the year 2003 show they are moving into North Carolina (378,963), Georgia (435,227), Tennessee

(123,838), South Carolina (95,076), Alabama (75,830), Kentucky (59,939), and Mississippi (39,569). In 2003, the south had approximately 1.2 million Mexican Latinos (Chapa & De La Rosa, 2004). Expansion extended into central/plains states as well: Arkansas (86,866), Kansas (188,252), Oklahoma (179,304), Nebraska (94,425), and Iowa (82,473). New growth expanded in the Great Lakes states to include Indiana (214,536), Wisconsin (192,921), and Minnesota (143,382). Similarly, expansion included the east cost, with Virginia (329, 540) and Delaware (37,277). Migration of Mexican ancestry populations went into Nevada (394, 970), Utah (201,559), and South Dakota (10,903) (Chapa & De La Rosa, 2004).

Latinos of Mexican origin can be divided into three major and one minor socioeconomic group: (1) low income, minimally skilled; (2) middle-class skilled workers; and (3) upper middle class, professionals. Group one is typically recent arrivals from Mexico who speak very little English and work as domestics in hotels, gardeners, car washers, waste collectors, meat packers, garment workers, and so on. More than one family may be living in one house (usually renting). Most of their relatives are still in Mexico, which may mean they will return periodically to Mexico to visit. They may also send money to help support the family. Group two is generally first- or second-generation born in the United States. They have a high school diploma and possibly community college experience or vocational/technical education. Their primary spoken language is English, but they still speak Spanish with their grandparents, parents, and relatives in Mexico. They are employed in skilled blue-collar jobs, such as auto assembly workers, entertainment industry workers, electricians or plumbers, and entry-level white-collar work, such as salespeople, office workers, and supermarket clerks. Over time in their careers, they move up the employment ladder (e.g., they become store managers, shift supervisors of office cleaning crews, and so on). As they advance employment-wise, they are able to purchase larger homes in suburbia. Group three is upper middle class, professionals. Typically, they are second- or third-generation Mexican Americans, are college educated, are in command of the English language, and may be literate in Spanish (i.e., read, write, and speak). They are employed as teachers, nurses, small business owners, middle-level managers in corporate America, and so on. At the upper end of this third group is an emerging small fourth group of high-income persons:

successful lawyers, engineers, CEOs, airline pilots, entertainers, and professional sports figures.

Among Latinos of Mexican ancestry, Spanish remains, for the majority, the dominant language. The less educated the Mexican American person is, the less he or she is knowledgeable in the use of the English language. This equation should not be a shock to anyone. However, what should be of surprise is how much English language understanding Mexican Americans acquire given the unsupportive conditions they find in schools. What this translates into is that Latino students who reach middle or high school are likely to be bilingual but not likely to be biliterate. This is to say, Mexican American secondary students are probably dominant in English and to a lesser degree speak Spanish. Typically, secondary Chicano students from low-income families are probably more fluent in the use of Spanish. Comparably, Chicano secondary students from middle-income families are less likely to speak Spanish. Spanish language usage in these two family types are influenced by parental language spoken and community language usage. Middle-income Mexican Americans are usually second-generation native born and live in housing developments that are integrated. Thus, there is less reliance on the use of Spanish in the home and in the neighborhood. Low-income families generally live in highly dense Mexican American communities where much of the business is transacted in Spanish ("Se habla Espanol") and where the home has grandparents who speak only Spanish.

The last variable (new attitude) that describes the diversity of the Mexican Latino population is the same that is appearing in other populations. New immigrants and succeeding generations are less willing to give up their cultural identities than were immigrants of the late 1800s and early 1900s. Part of creating this new attitude is the result of society's mellowing on the hard line; it is not necessary for total Americanization of immigrants. Two other factors that are promoting or at least allowing a wider understanding of cultural identity are technology and business. Due to technology, communication is now faster, easier, and cheaper. So immigrants in the United States can and do communicate in their native tongue via telephone and even the Internet on a frequent and regular basis. Second, more and more global and national corporations are employing persons who can and do relate to foreign countries as well as ethnic groups in the U.S. marketplace. In the case of Latinos of Mexican origin, these two factors are evident. First, many Mexican Latinos telephone extended family members in Mexico on a regular basis and wire funds estimated at 14.5 billion dollars annually! Second, because of NAFTA, more and more companies are producing goods in Mexico because of cheap labor costs. Within the U.S. border, Latinos, as consumers of products, are becoming a growing market. In 2003, it was reported that Latinos spent approximately $650 billion (Friedman, 2005). By the year 2010, it is projected that total personal income of U.S. Latino households will be $604 billion: $409 billion for Mexican Americans, $107 billion for Central/South Americans, $32 billion for Cuban Americans, and $56 billion for other Latinos (*Key Data: Hispanic Clout*, Knight Ridder/Tribune Information Services, 2004).

Referring to language usage, national advertisement, and the arts reinforces this point of a more permissive attitude of keeping cultural identity alive. In 1990, one in seven Americans spoke a language other than English at home, while in 2000 the U.S. Census Bureau reported that one in five Americans spoke another language. The 2000 Census found seven languages spoken in the United States by over a million people. Spanish was by far the language spoken the most (28.1 million people), followed in descending order by Chinese (2 million), French (1.6 million), German (1.3 million), Tagalog (1.2 million), and Vietnamese (1 million). All told about 47 million, or 20%, of Americans age five and older used a language other than English. In the advertisement world via television, newspaper, and radio, we see and hear Mexican food being promoted by fastfood chains and national markets (e.g., tortilla wraps, salsas, breakfast burritos at McDonald's). Also the auto industry and other national corporations are promoting their products and services in Spanish. The business sector continues to monitor not only the present conditions but the future as well. In the arts, we find a growing infusion of music—Latin beat in jazz, dances, and in film. Nuevo-Latino cooking is also finding its way into upscale restaurants.

CONCLUSION

There are three imperatives that argue forcibly for the design and creation of new schools for Latinos of Mexican origin: moral, social, and economic. The national and state policies imposed on schools produced a model and a set of practices that served the nation well, but not for this group or their schools. Given that significant changes are taking place and change is the future, schools must reconstitute themselves to prepare our nation's youths to function in the future. Plus the old schooling model will not serve the nation's future economic need.

The next chapter starts us on the road to conceiving new constructive schools. The context of the near future can be seen now; the obligations and tasks are in many ways greater and more complex, yet in some ways simple. In order for schools to fulfill their educational and community responsibilities in a more robust and effectual way, they will require more resources and must be organized differently and linked to other institutions in a more functional way. In short, schools cannot be viewed or treated as islands unto themselves. Particularly to successfully educate Latinos of Mexican origin, the entire village will need to be engaged.

NOTES

1. By the year 2050, it is projected that the U.S. population will be 49.9% white and 50.1% persons of color.

2. *School Board News* reported in the October 25, 2005, issue, page 5: "Although minorities made some gains in narrowing the achievement gap in recent years, many score gaps are not statistically different from what they were in 1992" (National School Board Association, 2005b).

3. In the early 1970s with the addition of a new special education designation, "learning disabled" (PL 91-230), more Latinos were assigned to special education programs.

4. American Indians have a higher dropout percentage than do Latinos but numerically have the smallest dropout numbers, whereas Latinos have the greatest dropout numbers of all groups.

5. However, Jewish and German parents provided instruction to their children via private after-school or weekend classes.

6. Each year, newspapers reporting on school board opinion polls substantiate this point. My own teaching experience in East Los Angeles verifies these annual surveys.

Chapter Two

It Takes an Entire Village

If the education of Latinos is to improve in the future, to the point that all students are learning at grade level, then public schools will have to be redefined and specifically tailored to match up with the traditional culture of Mexico and particularly the blended culture created by the Mexican American experience in the United States. By adopting a new educational philosophy toward the utilization of the Latino student's family culture, schools will need to be *transformed* so as to represent and incorporate this new cultural approach to teaching and learning. With the Latino family cultural approach as the epicenter, the transformed school will be able to attend to expanding its scope of usefulness, specifically to be a *full-service community institution*. While the redirection of purpose and new philosophy will require reorganization and new ways of doing things, the expansion of obligations and services will require more resources. The first part of restructuring will require acceptance of ideas and concepts already known but not included in past practices. The second part, to serve more constituents (beyond students) will, quite naturally, require more or at least adequate[1] resources. While the first part may appear the easier of the two, the second part can be just as simple to produce. Partnerships as a source of new support will be explored, as well as how professional associations and state and local agencies can be more cooperative than in the past. In short, this chapter addresses concepts new schools should be centered on, why their mission should be broadened, and how their support can be increased by tapping a greater variety of institutions.

WHY THE ENTIRE-VILLAGE CONCEPT?

The public school idea took shape during the creation of townships in the 1700s. Small rural communities put up buildings to provide services, such as a blacksmith barn where horses could be attended to; a general store where food and goods could be purchased and traded; a barber shop for shaves, hair cuts, and baths; a boarding house where people could sleep, eat, and drink; a church; and a jail. Later as a town got older, other services were added, such as a railroad station, telegraph office, survey office, doctor's office, and cemetery. As the town grew in size, the one-room schoolhouse was formed. For the most part, towns were homogeneous in makeup (i.e., people of like backgrounds and the same religion banded together). By the 1800s, the "common school" was born (Gutek, 2004). The common school was more than one room; it typically was a two-story building with multiple classrooms to accommodate graded classes arranged by student age.

As the nation grew in population, and towns grew into cities, the common school also grew to serve the town and surrounding farmlands and evolved into "neighborhood" schools. Neighborhood schools served the local residents (a smaller part of the big city) and remained connected by geographic proximity. As cities grew in complexity and organization, so did schools. Schools were divided beyond grades into elementary, junior high, and high schools, and the collection of schools was formed into a citywide district. The school district concept brought multiple schools under one governing board. Again, schools would mirror the neighborhoods. School personnel had the same values as the students and parents they served. During this time, city growth was due to the large influx of immigrants, mostly resettling from Europe. The increase in students coming from immigrant families caused cities to increase the high school grades from 10 to 12. Part of the rationale for adding more grades was to help in the "Americanization" of these foreigners (Suro, 1998). As society advanced from cities to metropolitan centers, large urban school districts where divided into subareas. Because unified school districts were getting too large in student numbers, school numbers, and geography, they moved to a decentralized approach. In order to manage the administrative component of the various schools and to try to keep to the concept of local control, school districts formed smaller geographic areas with a cluster of schools. These subareas had common population and economic characteristics. Decentralized school districts had one governing board, but administratively, each subdistrict was headed by an area superintendent and his or her administrative staff. With the advent of affordable cars and "freeways," suburbs were created. At first suburbs were simply bedroom communities and as such required only schools and places of worship on the weekends. Then as more services were created to provide support to residents, these communities became self-sufficient and soon moved to incorporate themselves into small municipal communities. As a result, school districts were created that matched these emerging city boundaries.

One organizational construct for decentralizing large urban school districts in metropolitan cities was to be able to allocate resources and account for responsibility. Underlining the decentralization movement was the thinking that size does matter. In order to manage such a large school district effectively, it had to be broken down into smaller units. In organizational terms, it is called "span and control." Regrettably, because schools are a by-product of society, the school leadership replicated society's bureaucratic nature and allowed the bureaucratic tenets to take priority over the democratic principle of knowing communities and serving these communities. Because of the U.S. economic evolution (haves and have nots), emergent political character (exclusion of certain groups such as women), and society's mental plague (racism), school personnel in certain parts of the district (usually in ethnic/racial minority neighborhoods) came to believe they knew better than the parents what was best for the students. As a result, schools in poor communities or in nonwhite neighborhoods did not get their fair share of the resources; school employees no longer believed they had to listen to community leaders and parents, or in short, they did not need to get to know or be accountable to the school's service population.

As the accountability movement of the 1990s has progressed, elected officials and educators have come to realize that schools must revert back to some principles that are constructive and help teachers cause learning among their students, schools to be of service to communities, and in turn, public education to advance society and strengthen people. This return to useful constructs is embedded in the entire-village concept. First and foremost, the village knows families and people as individuals (e.g., their family history, their particular problems and strengths, their comings and goings, their aspirations, their setbacks, and so forth). This knowledge of the entire school community is foremost because it creates within the educator a strong feeling of caring. This caring goes beyond wanting the student to learn to caring that the child succeeds not just in school but in life. By knowing and caring, school staff pass the sympathy stage and go to the empathic level. This mental passage is critical because it moves the teacher and administrator away from settling for less due to a "culture of poverty." Empathic teachers and principals find ways of helping their students overcome, whatever the obstacles!

The second construct is an enabler. In order for school staff to know and come to care about students and the neighborhoods in which they serve, schools must downsize. Size does matter in the classroom. In the case of schools, the common adage of "bigger is better" is false. It is a long-accepted conclusion that the student–teacher ratio directly influences the learning that takes place. The smaller the student–teacher ratio, the better the teacher will be able to provide tailored instruction to students. A report by the National Association of Secondary School Principals called *Breaking Ranks* (1996) cites the ills of high schools with student enrollments that number 2,000 or 3,000 or 4,000 or even 5,000! In the report, the NASSP calls for smaller high schools—no more than 600 students. But it is not only high schools that have grown far too large; elementary schools have grown as well to more than 1,000 students in some schools. The concept of school size will be visited later when increasing student learning and designing a school for better holding power and graduation rates are discussed.

The entire-village theme is the mental construct that will help create the new school concept. What follows is how this general premise should be applied to Latino communities and schools serving Mexican American Latinos specifically.

A MEXICAN AMERICAN CULTURALLY BASED SCHOOL PHILOSOPHY

The reader might ask, why is there a need for a Mexican culturally based school philosophy? After all, the common thinking of most people is these children will be living in the United States, where the language is English and the values are American. Furthermore, for the past 150 years, the schools have been the social agency where other immigrant groups have been successfully acculturated to become English-speaking Americans. The reply is twofold. First, the public schools have always had and continue to have a culturally based philosophy and curriculum. Both have been skewed to favor a white, European, Judeo-Christian value base. Groups whose ancestral experience and cultural background were similar to this WASP profile were able to adapt well to the school environment and way of doing things, and as such they were assimilated. In contrast, groups who are dissimilar to this white, European cultural base, such as Native Americans, African Americans, and Latinos, found the school acculturation experience too great a transformation, and thus their school experience was emotionally traumatic. This psychological transformation process interfered greatly with forming a strong self-concept and in turn distorted their learning process. Finally, even when these students of color adopted the acculturation process fully, after completing high school, society would not bestow on them equal benefits. As generations of Latinos passed through the process of school acculturation with society's marginal acceptance, younger brothers and sisters as well as children of previous graduates concluded it was not worth the effort, and dropping out was not all that bad. The employment prospects were not much better for a younger bother who graduated than for an older brother who dropped out of school.

The second reason for having a Mexican American culturally based school philosophy for Latinos of Mexican descent emerges from the first reply. That is, since schools are social agencies, built to resemble the society they are a part of, the values and norms (cultural elements) are endemic to them. Therefore, if the school culture either helps or impedes student learning, then it is logical to have students in an environment that is compatible with their home culture so as to capitalize on their learning strengths (Cardenas & Cardenas, 1972).

At the center of any group's culture is its language. Language brings to life the group's identity and concept of self. It is the means to express the various parts that make up the group's totality. It is not only the tool of communicating the culture but also the means of learning about all things. As such, language is more than a critical part of culture; it is a necessary tool that maintains and promotes group culture. Because of the vital function language provides to members of any culture, educators who were advocating in the 1960s for federal support of bilingual education were equally concerned with culture. In fact, Latino educators such as Sal Castro, a high school teacher in the Los Angeles Unified School District, who fought for the formation of a federally funded national bilingual educational program (Title VII), also deliberately wanted the term *bicultural education* included. Some of these educators[2] were more interested in the cultural component than just having bilingual teachers translate white, European cultural curriculum into Spanish. Educators knew the value of having the curriculum be relevant to the students. The common and simple example illustrating relevancy is best demonstrated by the annual telling of America's discovery by Christopher Columbus and leaving out any mention of the existence of American Indians in North America prior to Columbus's arrival. This traditional distortion by omission somehow is a contradiction in the minds of American Indian children, since they enter school with a different understanding as told to them by family members and their cultural history. Likewise, Mexican Latinos come to know prior to school entrance a different colonization and expansion of North America, not from New England westward but from Spaniards north from Mexico. For many Native American and Mexican American children, these conflicting stories become psychologically problematic.

The multicultural movement in education, brought into the forefront by the civil rights movement, is not just an effort based on promoting equity and appreciation of other cultures; it is founded on the cardinal principle that persons are prone to learn more when they can relate to the curriculum. That is, the more times students can find a connection between what is being taught and their lives, the more interesting and worthwhile the lesson will be. The primary goal of multicultural education is to help all students develop more positive attitudes toward different cultural, racial, ethnic, and religious groups (Banks, 1989). The assumption is that students with an understanding of their group's historical contributions will have a healthy self-concept of themselves, which will motivate individuals to achieve academically. Also, by seeing elements of their culture in other cultures, they will come to accept and appreciate other cultures. Equally, teachers, armed with honest information or the full story, could form a constructive attitude toward students of color. It is well known that teacher expectations for students determine to a large extent the amount and type (from memorization to inquiry to critical thinking) of learning by students (see Rosenthal & Jacobson, *Pygmalion in the Classroom*, 1992).

THE MODERN VILLAGE SCHOOL AUGMENTED BY OFFICIAL AGENCIES

At the start of this chapter, it was stressed that at the core of the transformation of schools serving Latino students was the need to incorporate Mexican ancestry, culture, and language. A close axiom to this fundamental educational philosophy is adopting a family attitude, and for Mexicans that means the entire extended family, including godparents. So schools should follow suit. What is meant by the incorporation of extended family concept into schools? Besides fulfilling its mission of teaching students, schools should extend their primary mission to become full-service institutions. School facilities should be used after school hours and on weekends. Because of physical proximity to homes, schools in poor communities are typically one of the few places where residents can go to get public services. Therefore, these schools should be used to the maximum. Currently, most of these schools are overcrowded. So it is not proposed that we increase the burden on these institutions. Instead, with the expanded service concept, schools should partner with municipal agencies. Recently, cities are getting more involved with public school districts. Mayors of cities are lending their leadership, and accordingly, governmental involvement is increasing. The city of Chicago is a good example. As a reminder, Chicago has had a large Mexican American population since the early 1900s (migrant workers went north to pick crops and stayed). In 2000, the Latino population in Chicago was 753,644, or 26% (U.S. Census Bureau, 2000). As Chicago has done, cities can offer help with after-school and weekend recreation through the parks and recreation department. City services could be dispensed at schools by having city representatives setting up shop two or three days a week or a few hours each day. The cities can and should pay schools for use of their space. To reduce the crowded space issues, these services can be held after school hours and on weekends. In large urban centers, cities are adding staff responsible for developing city-funded educational programs. Such city programs are aimed at providing greater assistance or support to schools.

They range from acting as brokers to get businesses to "adopt a school," to running mentoring programs (facilitating students to get help on the telephone with homework), to partially underwriting reading programs with city funds. The city of Phoenix is another good example where city staff and budgets have been in place to help schools since the 1990s. There are other major cities with longer involvement as well.

State education departments are criticized by most schools because of the state's regulatory function. But there is growing pressure, mainly by the federal government through the accountability (reform) movement, for state departments to be service operations. These services should include providing schools with school test results, helping school personnel interpret student test results (diagnosis), and providing state-appointed teams to help schools align curriculum.

Along with getting the state department to offer useful services instead of being a monitor of progress or lack thereof, it is recommended that schools develop relationships with local colleges or universities to provide ongoing, coherent staff development. Not just four-year colleges but two-year community colleges as well. And within the universities, not just colleges of education but across disciplines, such as business, nursing, fine arts, Chicano studies, and so on. But schools should look beyond these typical sources of expertise. Here is an opportunity to look to the Mexican American community, to become a resource, to be viewed as experts that can share information about the Spanish language, local histories, insight into motivating parents to get more involved, and more. (Parental involvement will be discussed in later chapters.)

Besides city and state agencies and local colleges and universities, there is federal assistance, mostly in the form of supplemental funds. Since the start of the accountability movement, there has been a quiet minority view to reject federal involvement, since public education is a state responsibility. However, since the start of the 21st century and No Child Left Behind (NCLB), educators—including state legislators—are now publicly voicing their reluctance to take federal dollars because of the heavy requirements, or better stated, hard restrictions. Also, local leaders have discovered that federal assistance has not been equal to the federal mandates. Nonetheless, the federal government, like many others, is looking to support good ideas. One idea that has gained favor recently within the federal government is the previously mentioned concept of designing schools to be culturally based. For example, the federal Bureau of Indian Affairs (BIA), beginning with President Clinton's administration, is working with Indian tribes to construct or remodel BIA schools to reflect and respect their culture. This approach is a 180-degree shift from the one adopted by the BIA when it first started (1880s) to create Indian schools.[3] The underlying belief is that building schools that are culturally sensitive will influence the Indian students positively and improve Indian education. The Bush administration proposed $292 million during its annual 2004 budget request to design six or seven Indian schools each year (Gehrke, 2003).

THE BUSINESS SECTOR AS A PARTNER IN CREATING COMMUNITY SCHOOLS

"We're all in this mess together." So says actor Gregory Peck in the 1961 film *Guns of Navarone*. This quote is applicable today when thinking about public education. In fact, the 1983 U.S. Department of Education report, titled *A Nation at Risk*, equated public education as under siege and at risk of losing the war. Just as the nation mobilized all home-front efforts to win Word War I and World War II, so we in education have to mobilize all sectors too. The good news is that educators do not have to convince the business sector that it is in their best interest to be a partner in revitalizing public schools. Business leaders across the country have learned that in order for them to be competitive and successful (in the short and long run), schools must prepare a better educated and technologically skilled workforce. Further, businesses are for the most part looking into the future in order to be ahead of the curve. Part of their future agenda is knowing the makeup of the nation's population. They know that the future consumers of goods and employees will be persons of color. Bellwether states such as California and New York show today what tomorrow will be. This understanding is not held by corporate America alone but also by small businesses.

Two other historical events help bring business and education together. During the 1980s, corporate America was in a crisis. With the emergence of technology, the economy became interdependent and global. As a result, not only did competition become greater, but how work got done changed substantively as well. Thus U.S. corporations at first had to downsize and restructure their operations in order to survive. But they realized the challenge was more complex. So they had to *rethink* how to conduct their affairs. The business community, out of necessity, transformed itself from being a "closed" organization to an "open" one (i.e., businesses looked outward to assess the external situation and particularly what their clients or consumers wanted or needed). Following this movement, particularly in the 1990s, businesses began the entrepreneurial stage. Concurrent with the business transformation, school districts in our metropolitan centers were undergoing student growth and consequently taking on the characteristics of industrial business America—the model that modern corporate America was shedding! As an example, the Los Angeles Unified School District is struggling to serve approximately 746,000 students (72% are Hispanic) in 806 schools (the majority of which were constructed prior to the 1960s) with 80,325 employees. The budget was $13.3 billion, larger than some rural states in America (LAUSD web page). The same could be said of other school districts in other major urban centers, such as New York, Chicago, Atlanta, Dallas, Denver, San Francisco, and Miami. The similarities in profile between large urban school districts and corporate America are many. But one characteristic is particularly important for a future relationship. Leaders, in both sectors, could not only understand each others' plight because of their similar profiles but more important could also appreciate each others' status and as such could come to see each other as equal partners, partners whose future fates were linked with each other, specifically schools providing businesses with their workforce.

With these understandings as a baseline, school building principals as well as district superintendents should be more aggressive in extending their scope of work to connect on an ongoing basis with local business leaders to form partnerships of all kinds. These partnerships can result in bringing additional resources to schools to do things that state funds are inadequate to do. Beyond the much-needed financial or material resources, a business partnership can yield a valuable conceptual component. What is this more important asset? School leaders can learn from business leaders how to transform schools in at least five ways: (1) in thinking (to attend to annual operations but also to the future agenda), (2) in designing (how people should work as a unit to maximize resources), (3) in building (facilities shape worker and learner attitudes), (4) in providing service (forming relationships with students and parents), and (5) in improving the final product (delivery of teaching via equipment and curriculum). However, a strong word of caution is necessary. Educators are not being asked to adopt the business mind-set when it comes to teachers providing instruction and students learning. Efficiency and productivity should not dictate learning, service, and environment. Nor should business executives assume they should become the senior partners in this relationship and dictate what school CEOs should do. While school leaders are responsible for "running" a large and complex enterprise as administrators, it must be kept clear in their minds that they are educators first and that schools are dedicated to developing the minds, spirits, and bodies of young persons. As such, each student must be treated in ways consistent with their upbringing, not uniformly like raw material or inanimate objects.

PROFESSIONAL ASSOCIATIONS AS GOOD NEIGHBORS

There is a wide range of professional educational associations. One type is formed to advance the interest of a particular group. Examples are the National Education Association (NEA), American Federation of Teachers (AFT), National Association of Secondary School Principals (NASSP), and American Association of School Administrators (AASA). However, another type of professional association has been formed with the primary intent to promote a particular discipline (e.g., National Council of Teachers of Mathematics). A third type of association comes under the umbrella of advocacy, such as the Council of Great City Schools. Within these three types, there are professional associations that match up well with affairs of Latino schools. Just to identify a few, in type one there is the Association of Mexican American Educators (AMAE) in California; in type two there is the National Association for Bilingual Education (NABE); and in type three there is the Intercultural Development Research Association (IDRA) in Texas. Even more in number, and therefore creating a greater capacity for getting more assistance, are the professional associations' official caucuses, or subgroups of experts and interests. These caucuses are composed of like members (e.g., Latino superintendents within AASA) who promote the interests of that particular group (e.g., school districts with majority Latino students).

These national and state associations have grown in number and more important are examining pressing issues and problems facing students of color and publishing reports of their findings. Most of the reports do a good job of stating the current status, identifying reasons that likely contribute to the problem, and proposing broad recommendations of what might be or needs to be done to overcome the status quo. By providing this service, they provide ideas and direction to school practitioners. For most practitioners, this service of information sharing (via reports) does not find its way into the minds of educators. Similarly, professional associations hold annual conferences, where experts present information about current national trends, problems, and programs. Because school district funds are limited, most practitioners are unable to attend such conferences. Finally, these professional organizations provide information by way of their publications (journals), but again, most public school educators do not read these regularly printed materials.

So, there is a rich resource, called professional associations, that is not being utilized on a broad enough level or scope. What schools need to do to help themselves more is to utilize these services with much more frequency and with more practicality. How? First, identify professional associations that mirror the schools' needs and concerns. For example, NABE and Teachers of English as a Second Language (TESL) are specific to language development for English language learners. Also, the Council of Great City Schools targets its efforts toward schools that have high concentrations of students of color. (To state the obvious, almost all big cities now have the student profile of the Council of Great City Schools.) Second, develop action plans that will ensure that large numbers of school instructional staff will have regular access to written reports and association journals, as well as attend annual conferences on a rotating basis. Those not able to attend can receive information by attendees and the opportunity to discuss the sessions.

What is being proposed is the creation of a meaningful staff development plan—a plan with a coherent school focus rather than an individual, fragmented approach; a plan that covers more than one year; and a plan that requires continuous participation by staff. Professional associations at times offer fresh and usually relevant ideas, and schools should take advantage of these associations by providing a structured opportunity for dialogue and implementation of ideas.

CONCLUSION

The message in this chapter is twofold. First, to truly educate Latino youths of Mexican ancestry, a new and positive mind-set must be internalized by all the education community involved—school board members, administrators, counselors, teachers, and clerical and support staff. This mind-set must accept that the Mexican culture has value. The school must respect and incorporate this culture, including the use of the Spanish language. The fundamental belief that every child wants to learn must be set in place as a given. Connected to this belief, teachers in particular must believe it is possible and imperative to find a teaching style that matches the students' learning habits. The current old-school paradigm with patchwork specialized programs does not work sufficiently. Thus, a new model needs to be installed. The new model must begin with smaller sized schools to have a sense of community. Second, these newly designed schools must extend their services beyond just teaching students to learn; they must provide assistance to parents and community groups. New thinking and doing more than the traditional teaching will require more resources—not just money but also human resources. In order to gain access to additional resources, partnerships need to be formed; networks with professional organizations must be established; and staff development must become a central, ongoing responsibility instead of the peripheral and occasional service it has experienced.

The next part of the book, chapters 3 and 4, will unfold with more specificity the utility of internalizing and maintaining this much-needed new mind-set into schools. One of the major reasons for engendering a new positive mind-set by all school personnel is that it will be the primary source of human energy. Most school personnel in low-income communities get burned out fast, become disappointed with the returns (too little) for the amount of effort they put out (extensive), and are dissatisfied with how the general public thinks of their work. Hence, new hope must be instilled in the minds of school people. With new hope comes their new source of energy. Second, once greater hope is sustained, then schools will need to be organized to promote liberated teachers and more flexible and creative administrators. Structure by way of horizontal communication, team relationships, and role responsibility will have to be put into place to expand opportunity and yield success.

NOTES

1. To date, adequate funding has not been provided. In September 2004, an Austin, Texas, court judge ruled that state funding was insufficient. This ruling came 30 years after the famous Rodriguez case started in San Antonio, Texas, which challenged the state funding formula as being insufficient and unfair.

2. Dr. Juan Aragon, an education professor at the University of New Mexico at the time, was a strong believer in the bicultural component as well.

3. The name "Office of Indian Affairs" was changed in 1974 to BIA. The 1880s were known as the assimilation era.

Part II

NEW MIND-SET, GREATER ENERGY, AND NEW ROLES

The way we view the world determines how we behave in organizational roles and in turn how the organization functions and achieves its mission. Since schools for Latinos must be reconceived and redesigned to operate differently than in the past, principals, teachers, counselors, and all school staff will, out of necessity, need to erase old and dysfunctional models and put in their place new mind-sets. Another critical reason why a new mind-set must be substituted is that teaching and learning are fundamentally two interconnected activities that become human endeavors. The human energy that powers this basic function in schools must be increased and rechanneled. The development of school staff has traditionally been done through in-service training. Chapter 3 discusses what staff development training must address in order to develop fresh and positive ways of thinking, to help staff undertake their roles in more constructive and productive ways, and more important to create a school community of believers. Many interested stakeholders want to believe that the teaching workforce of today is calling for more information that helps them understand students of color better and permits them to fulfill their responsibilities in a more satisfying way by getting students to achieve more than before.

Energizing school staff is one important way of building capacity, but more is necessary if these new Latino community-based schools are going to be successful in reaching their expanded mission of being full-service centers. Two other ways of increasing school capabilities are discussed: utilizing technology and forming partnerships. Schools will need to get smarter in utilizing technology, which offers versatility, speed, and minimum personnel and can now make individualized instruction truly possible and self-learning practical, as well as make many school duties manageable. While most Latino schools are typically underfunded, old, and overcrowded—and require more resources and assistance than their sister suburban schools—they have for the most part equitable access to technology. However, in the other resource areas, they are not, for example, in workbooks, computer software programs, or current textbooks. And because they are not, new Latino schools will have to reach out to be supported in much greater ways than before. Thus in chapter 4, we propose that in order to get more support, Latino schools will need to raise their learning goals for students and expand their mission to be full-service schools, not just to students but to the community. By enlarging their circle of responsibility to help families and community-based organizations, schools will see that they will attract a larger workforce of volunteers. But schools will have to learn to reach out in different ways than in the past. Schools will need to offer respect and earn the trust of persons who have been excluded in the past. In short, they must become flexible, work differently, be able to adapt to new ways, and change how they engage with the community in order to develop equitable relationships.

Chapter Three

Engendering New Hope: *Sí se puede!*

Since teaching and learning are fundamentally human endeavors (typically between an adult and youths in public schools), it is critical and essential that the educator and the student have the proper mind-set—an attitude toward each other that promotes formal instruction to occur in order to fulfill an even greater accomplishment, the goal of human growth. But once a new mind-set is adopted, it is imperative that a new school paradigm be put into effect, if for no other reason than we are at the start of a new millennium. But more important, a new paradigm must be adopted because we cannot continue to use a model that was created more than 100 years ago that produced too few positive outcomes. Clearly, society has undergone a transformation and so must schools in order to prepare future generations for success. It is important that attention be given to creating and maintaining a positive mind-set, particularly in schools where there is typically a different composition than in middle-class suburbia. The teaching workforce is typically white, female, and monolingual English speaking, coming from middle-class families living in suburbia. However, most Latino students of Mexican ancestry come from low-income families, an inner-city experience, and a Spanish-speaking environment (to varying degrees). To underscore this mismatch between a white teacher workforce and rainbow-colored student body, a profile of school districts in central Arizona, which is a good representation of what is happening in metro centers across the country, is provided (see Table 3.1).

In examining Table 3.1, the highest difference between white teachers and minority students is 62%. The Phoenix high school district is an inner-city district. Furthermore, more than 90% of its 86% "minority"

Table 3.1. Percentages of Minority Teachers to Minority Students

	Teachers		Students		
School District	**Number**	**Minority**	**Number**	**Minority**	**Difference**
Chandler Unified	1,600	10%	27,000	42%	32%
Deer Valley Unified	1,850	2%	32,000	20%	18%
Gilbert Public Schools	2,100	7%	35,400	23%	16%
Mesa Public School	4,400	12%	75,000	40%	28%
Paradise Valley Unified	2,100	5%	35,000	25%	20%
Peoria Unified	2,000	8%	36,600	27%	19%
*Phoenix Union	1,500	24%	23,000	86%	62%
Scottsdale Unified	1,600	6%	26,300	19%	13%
Tempe Union	800	9%	13,300	37%	28%

Notes: This table also shows that minority students rarely have the benefit of being taught by a person of their race or ethnicity. Difference in percentages is between minority teacher and minority student. Percentages are estimated because teachers are self-reporting ethnicity. Original source of reporting is individual school district.
*Phoenix is an inner-city school (greatest difference), while the others are suburban.
Source: Arizona Republic, Teachers: Giving Back to Alma Mater, 2004.

students (now the majority) are Hispanic and more than 95% of these Hispanics are of Mexican ancestry. To extend the profile to the school level, one high school, Carl Hayden, has 2,350 students, 97% of whom are nonwhite. Of these students of color, 92% are Latino, including 62% who live in monolingual Spanish-speaking homes.

Three major differences (race, income, and social experience) create a wider distance than normal between white teacher and brown children than the typical white middle-class teacher in suburban schools with white students. Thus the current school paradigm, created in the late 1800s to Americanize white immigrants from Europe, fits white middle-class society but not communities of color from Latin America or the Far East. Added to this personal characteristic mismatch are the various modes of teaching methods used, observations, practicums, and student teaching. Typically the teacher preparation programs in most colleges of education (especially those removed from urban centers) revolve around white middle-class student populations or schools. In teacher preservice programs, there is limited time available to provide information about inner-city schools or students of color. Because of these reasons, we start with developing and nurturing a new and more conducive mind-set and then follow with transforming schools to create a new design and learning environment.

A NEW MIND-SET FOR EDUCATORS AND STUDENTS

What should be the new mind-set for both teachers and Latino students? What should the catchphrase be? We've heard many in the past decade: All kids can learn! Well, all kids want to learn, especially when they start school. Their interest in learning will continue if they find success. But it must be more than a slogan; it must be sincere in the mind and taken to heart. When it is taken seriously, it works. The best example of what this new mind-set can produce is seen in the experience of historically black colleges and universities. Originally, black faculty instructing black students believed in their students' ability and desires. The faculty had similar experiences growing up, and thus there was a mutual understanding about history and current conditions. There was a common and realistic respect between instructor and student. A current example of the new mind-set is found in the Reverend Jesse Jackson's program. He launched a nationwide program for African American students with the phrase "I am somebody." This statement was expressed on a daily basis. He along with many African American educators concluded that the majority of public educators and African American students and parents had succumbed to the false belief that black students could not achieve or did not want to achieve in school. Another example of the importance of instilling a positive concept is found in the work of Jim Brown, the famous Cleveland Browns running back and a graduate of Syracuse University. When he works with black youths, he stresses to them and those working with them to develop a strong concept of self, first and foremost.

Again, the need to instill this new mind-set is critical because of the demographics. Nationally, 39% of the student body is made up of nonwhite populations. Only 16% of the teachers are persons of color (National Center for Education Statistics, 2005). The demographic projections indicate that students of color will continue to increase, since birthrates are higher and family size is larger than for white families. Also, schools of education will not be able to keep up with the ever-increasing demand for new teachers (due in part to teacher retirement, turnover, and student increase), let alone attract a more diversified teaching workforce. And in metropolitan areas, the ratio of students of color to white teachers is even more imbalanced. As educators, we also must remember that teaching is a *sociocultural-based process*, not just an approach based on subject matter and methodology.

It is important that students internalize a strong belief about themselves because inner-city youths or students of color acquire a defeatist attitude after a short time in school. In fact, by the sixth grade many students of color in poor neighborhood schools come to lose hope! Not just about doing well in school but also about having a promising future. They feel they can't make it because there are too many forces against them. The signals come from television programs, movies, newspapers, magazines, advertisements, and the media in general. To counteract these subtractors of hope, we must engender on a daily basis not just by words but also by our actions that we believe in them, that we care about them, more than just as students—as persons. We must show that we care by talking about their interests outside of class, being approachable on matters other than just class assignments, and talking to them about the social and economic realities of their present and future. The American Dream is theirs to be had, but not solely by applying themselves; they must stay alert. Expressing a true sense of caring should be easy, especially for teachers, yet in ways it is inhibited by institutions. College of education programs teach prospective teachers to be objective, to distance themselves from their pupils so as to create respect and maintain discipline. Teachers are cautioned not be social workers. The teachers' time should be spent on preparing lesson plans and gaining more knowledge about what they teach, their subject matter. However, human development is more than just formal learning about subject matter, and instruction of pupils is more than lesson plans and what takes place within the classroom.

For children or youths to grow as self-sufficient persons, they must know more than facts and information pieces or a process to solve problems. They must learn to judge character, value principles, demonstrate ethics, form and nurture relationships, be contributing members to local communities, and more. Hence, subject-matter teachers as well as elementary teachers must see themselves as responsible for knowing the student in class as well as understanding the pupil as a person, a member of a family, and a part of the local community who is subject to society's forces. To fulfill their role as teachers, they must care and believe in each and every student as an individual.

Teachers must translate this new belief into having high expectations, rather than making excuses for not being able to teach Latino students better. This may and probably does mean more work because they will need to think about how to reach these students, students they are not fully prepared to teach because their formal preparation program did not include instruction of diverse children and youths. After adopting the concept that all kids can learn, teachers must then adopt a corollary axiom—"I can teach anyone." Classroom teachers and school building principals will need to seek out knowledge about pedagogy, curriculum, and management from technical assistant centers, from federally funded education labs, through their own readings, by attending professional association conferences, and by other means.

In chapter 4, more specificity will be provided on what teachers must do differently. Following are the items to be discussed: incorporating home language and other cultural elements in the curriculum, doing adequate and continual assessment of student progress, reaching out to parents on a regular basis, and recognizing and treating students as individuals and not just as group members. Principals will need to create open schools, where parents and community persons are welcomed and sought after to be in the schools.

This new positive belief about students should be adopted schoolwide, not just by teachers and school administrators but also by support staff—custodial workers, cafeteria employees, bus drivers, and others. This new spirit needs to be exhibited in classrooms as well as in hallways, in offices, and throughout the campus. The school climate must be welcoming, encouraging, upbeat, and most of all representative of the Latino culture, certainly by using and incorporating the Spanish language and other components such as foods, music, and art, as well as recognizing and celebrating Mexican holidays such as Cinco de Mayo.

NEW STRUCTURE

With the new mind-set in place across the school, a new source of energy will be tapped. The human spirit is elevated when motivated by the mind

and strengthened by the heart. If we believe in something and have a goal
to reach, then we will find the energy to apply ourselves. We will replenish our thinking and action if we can see progress. Advancement will be
made if we harness our efforts in the right way. We must have flexibility
to make adjustments, we must have openness to create options, and we
must have means to implement plans and actions based on data, not just
feelings. Hence we need to reengineer schools into learning organizations,[1] where the infrastructure fits Latino communities.

The new mind-set within educators must include another dimension: As
professionals, they must adopt the thinking of being a change agent. The
responsibility for changing schools befalls both teacher and administrator.
In broad strokes, the change agent mentally must have three tenets. One,
in order to be meaningfully effective, schools must move away from an
ethnocentric focus to a culturally pluralistic philosophy. Two, schools
must redirect their major time and energy from changing the student (to
fit the school paradigm) to changing the "system" to extract the best from
Latino communities to help the student and the school. Three, because
there is a wide separation between the Latino of Mexican Ancestry experience and the school model, we can no longer continue to use the "add-
on" approach (i.e., developing special programs for "these" students). The
special project approach is akin to the pullout system (e.g., a monolingual
Spanish-speaking student is pulled out of class for an hour or two a day to
learn English, and the remaining four or five hours are back in a "regular"
classroom). Again the add-on approach is focused on getting the student
to change instead of making the school over to provide adequate instruction so that the student learns. Even when the add-on approach does create a moderate change in school, it only alters one part of the model, not
the entire model. For this reason, many advocates for change argue for
systemic change, deep and comprehensive change. Just as giant corporations in U.S. business went to reengineering and restructuring to the point
of abandoning high efficiency (low-cost production, strategic marketing,
and higher prices) to making the entrepreneurial approach king (survey-
ing customer needs, analyzing changing times, and creating new products), so too must schools undergo similar transformations.

Having a new mind-set will force us to transform schools to permit and
facilitate a new way of doing things. Schools will be seen in a new light,
not as tradition-bound agencies. The old policies, out-of-step practices,

and counterproductive arrangements will be seen as incompatible with Latino youths and communities. The current school model may serve white students well, but it does not serve students with a different culture and language. In the past, and to a large extent at this time, schools wanted students to change and fit the school's cultural mold of a homogeneous America. For white students this is not a big problem. They rebel somewhat, but for them the changes are minor adoptions. For many students of color, this refitting and makeover of themselves is significant and traumatic. It is this psychological remake that interferes with learning and prevents a strong self-concept. Latino students are forced to attend to two agendas simultaneously while in school. One is the acculturation agenda, and the other is the formal learning agenda. Acculturation has meant to put all aspects of the mother culture secondary to the American profile. This secondary status has been accomplished by the schools either indirectly or overtly, communicating that ancestral culture (including language) is of little value and in fact may be detrimental. Hence, Latino students are pushed to harbor shame toward their culture. In so doing, they begin to have doubts about their abilities. In the absence of too few positives, a general negative results.

In order for school personnel to counteract this endemic practice, they will have to redesign and redefine how they are organized and what their purposes are. What do we mean by transforming schools? First, schools cannot be managed as bureaucracies. Standardization, a school term substituted for bureaucracy, promotes an overreliance on uniformity, allows no or few exceptions, follows procedure over the more important question of relevance, guards routine, discourages inquiry, and resists change. Second, in place of bureaucracy, schools should become learning organizations as proposed by Peter Senge in his 1994 book *The Fifth Discipline: The Art and Practice of the Learning Organization*. Third, human capital is valued as the greatest resource. Teachers and administrators, along with other professional staff, are encouraged and rewarded for continuing to enhance their abilities, and in turn, their capacity to work effectively is increased commensurately. Places where school administrators organize formal programs for their teaching staff to extend their understanding—not just about teaching and learning but also about the students who attend the school as well as the community—are more vibrant and personally appealing places in which to work. These are schools where stereotypical thinking is questioned. Fourth, when traditional boundaries are erased (i.e., within the school), grade levels do not separate teachers from one another, and classrooms do not isolate teachers from one another. Additionally, these are places where parents and community persons can provide lessons for learning both away from the campus as well as on the campus. In short, new Latino schools will require expansive thinking and behavior tied more to current effective practices than to the early 20th-century paradigm.

NEW FUNCTION AND ROLE

As part of this transformation by way of a new infrastructure, new schools for Latino youths of Mexican descent will need to reconceive their mission and take on a new role of doing things. First, schools will have to be expanded to become full-service agencies. Besides just providing formal instruction to students, schools should become places where municipal services are provided, limited health services are available, job training and placement are offered, English-language instruction is given to adults for workplace advancement, family assistance is accessible, community functions are held, adults can continue to gain new knowledge, and recreation to community groups is offered. This means that the facilities must be accessible after school and on weekends. With the expansion of the mission, and to counterbalance the additional load, schools will need to help themselves instead of relying on inadequate resources.[2] In the next chapter we describe how this may be accomplished, especially at a time when future school enrollments of Latinos are predicted to increase. Second, to carry out this expanded function, schools will need to carry out responsibilities through a new role, the entrepreneurial approach. That is, schools must depend upon themselves to be more resourceful. To be entrepreneurial, schools will need to allow for flexibility, promote variety in doing things, engender big and small inquiry, facilitate experimentation and innovation, assist in the collection of information, insist that decisions are based on data and discussion, and encourage community building and interaction among internal school groups and external community groups. Such matters are typically the domain of school administration. However, change in the magnitude of transformation requires administrators to act more as leaders than as managers, and school leaders must act in partnership with both teachers and community groups.

Transformation requires additional resources, not just reallocation of existing budget amounts. As we know all too well, schools in Latino communities are inadequately funded already. So these schools cannot depend upon the traditional state funding source. Schools will, out of necessity, need to form partnerships with local community groups for expertise, with small businesses for tutors and mentors, with big businesses for donations, with community colleges and universities for technical support, and with others as well.

Leadership for transformational change means working to create a new climate where persons feel secure enough to *imagine* and to question traditional convention. Trust is formed so that persons feel they can propose and try new ways of doing things without doing harm to students, where community building and group action is valued, so persons can engage with one another and volunteering becomes the norm. In this new role, the school leadership is more concerned with the mental hygiene of the staff and students rather than the inner workings of the school (e.g., schedules). This is so because it will be the mental constructs of authenticity, commitment to goals, belief in one another, valuing group life, and encouraging learning that will create an attitude of efficacy and a willingness to be innovative.

OUTLINE OF NEW CULTURALLY CENTERED SCHOOLS

Schools, particularly those located in wealthy communities, have begun to adopt the "learning organizational" model. Public school systems, such as in Chicago, are moving to incorporate some elements described previously, driven by the federal government's accountability initiative, NCLB. Within this broad learning organizational framework, schools for Latinos of Mexican ancestry must be stamped totally with a cultural embossment.

Experience with developing and evaluating instructional programs for limited-English-proficient students has provided educators with understanding about what is necessary for English language learners to be successful in school. It is from this program knowledge base that the following school characteristics are offered.

Creating a culturally sensitive schoolwide climate is important. By now the reader should be convinced that students of color in general and Latino youths in particular do not perform well in schools that deny them their ethnic or racial identity. Programs where their language is used and other cultural elements are incorporated into the curriculum are better received and reinforce a sense of well-being. Furthermore, because there are different Latino students (e.g., recent immigrant, first generation, non-English speaker, limited English speaker), there needs to be a Latino cultural base and varying degrees of language usage. The measurement level must be that the students, parents, and community sense the school does value its culture and language honestly.

The importance and value of teaching children about their culture and in their mother tongue are seen not only through past efforts (Germans and Jews) but also by recent efforts, namely the Hawaiians. According to a 1983 survey, it was estimated that only 1,500 people who remained on the Hawaiian Islands spoke Hawaiian. As a result of efforts by parents, immersion programs were begun in public schools at both the elementary and secondary level. In 2005, the Hawaiian State Department of Education reports that there are 19 sites with language immersion programs and 4 at public charter schools. Today, there are approximately 6,000 to 8,000 Hawaiian speakers throughout the state (Staton, 2005).

Culturally knowledgeable, change-oriented, and secure leadership is a must. Since what happens in a school district or the local schools depends on the district superintendent or building principal, these persons must be culturally knowledgeable advocates of change for student growth and community development. As we know, these two positions are significant because of the tone these individuals set and decisions they make with regard to personnel and programs. Superintendents and principals must be more experienced and knowledgeable than others if public education is to advance and be effective for communities. With the advent of the information age, no individual can keep up with the knowledge explosion or be an expert in all curricula and pedagogies as well as finances, law, strategic planning, and more. Therefore, it becomes more imperative that these individuals be secure with themselves and not threatened by others who are specialists and have more knowledge in a particular area. By being secure with their own abilities, principals and superintendents can recruit, identify, and hire persons who are open to creativity, who question ineffectiveness, who are receptive to change, and who believe they are enriched by learning about other cultures and languages. By amassing a professional staff, whether it is at the district level or school site, they are forming a community of believers—personnel who believe that every student counts, that no child is expendable, and that the true measure of success is student accomplishment. In short, a child-centered philosophy focused on the whole child evolves.

Community building is important and necessary. School leaders must internalize that student success and school advancement will occur not through individual effort but through group action. The school is a community within a community, not a location where people routinely gather within a set time throughout the year. When schools start thinking of themselves as communities, they should perceive themselves as a part of a larger local community, not a separate group that needs persons to build bridges with the greater community or its subgroups. By seeing themselves as one, the resources they can call upon become greater. Instead of schools having to sell a particular venture to parents, community groups, and agencies, these community partners will already have a stake in the undertaking and a high level of buy-in. Most important, parents in particular will no longer be considered distant, unknown, separate, unwilling, or difficult to communicate with. On the contrary, parents will be understood because "neighbors" talk to each other on a regular basis. In so doing they get to know about each other directly, founded on facts and firsthand information. The information is current and not based on myth or old misconceptions. Communities make decisions based on information rendered by interested parties. In so doing consensus develops, leading to a feeling of equal worth.

Cultural classrooms become operational. Individual perception and understanding are colored by one's experience or group culture. In the Mexican culture, family is central. This translates into a variety of discrete ways of thinking, behaving, and responding. One belief is that the family is greater than any one person. Cooperation is promoted, not individual effort. In school, individual effort is the rule, and teamwork is secondary. In terms of behavior, children are to be respectful to all adults, and obedience to parents is paramount. However, how families demonstrate these beliefs and behaviors at home is different from how school teachers expect their American students to behave. Therefore, teachers must learn about parenting in the Mexican culture (e.g., the father's role versus the mother's role) instead of schools trying to teach Mexican American parents how to be "good parents" (i.e., how they should support their children while they are in school, or more correct, what teachers want/need parents to do).

The critical points of this chapter were recently captured in the local section of a Phoenix newspaper. In a short article titled "Mexican Consul Offers Boost to Parents, Kids: Official Visits 'Failing' School," the consul general was quoted as saying, "Education is something that should be looked at as an investment, . . . and where there is a deficit, we should pay special attention." A reaction by a parent was, "We should inculcate in [our children] to be someone, to keep studying so they can have the things that people in Mexico don't have." A school official talked about the importance for children to continue to speak Spanish at home while mastering other languages such as English. Last, the consul general reminded parents that they should not forget their roots: "Other segments of society are allowed to feel proud of their ancestry. Mexicans have this perception that they have to . . . renounce their culture or heritage" (Alonzo-Dunsmoor, 2005, B5).

CONCLUSION

With a new positive mind-set as their foundation, schools will necessarily have to expand their mission and role. This will require creating a new infrastructure, nothing short of transformation. These new schools will be community and culturally centered; as such, they will need to change organizationally, operationally, and conceptually. The next chapter expands on some of these changes with more specificity and shares ideas on how to generate much-needed capacity and resources.

NOTES

1. This book goes beyond designing effective programs that help special populations achieve success in school achievement. It aims to redefine schools (more than the instruction programs) to be successful with the entire school population, in this case Mexican American. The focus of the book is not on rural schools and migrant students.

2. A word of caution: I know well that true adequacy will be long in coming. Even now (2006), many school districts that were awarded more funds by winning inequity court cases are still "playing catch-up" with the adequacy criterion.

Chapter Four

Building Capacity
and Creating Flexibility

The previous chapters have expressed from various perspectives why it is necessary to substantially redefine schools that serve all kinds of Mexican American students (e.g., recent arrivals from Mexico, first-generation born in the United States, middle income, inner city) and communities. A different set of mental constructs has been shared that educators should believe in and that are necessary for schools to implement in order to be successful. This chapter concentrates on laying out another set of practical requirements that must be in place both prior to the remaking and during the operating of these new community schools. These new practical requirements are enablers. Specifically, these enablers will enlarge capacity and create more flexibility. They are (1) building capacity through continual staff development, (2) using and incorporating technology, and (3) forming partnerships.

Before proceeding to the discussion of these enablers, it would be valuable to state the argument for promoting the transformation of schools, other than what is taking place now under the reform movement banner No Child Left Behind. In broad strokes, the historical education of Latinos of Mexican descent in the United States can be divided into four stages. In stage one (1800–1950s), the main purpose of schools was to "Americanize" students of Mexican descent, as was the intent with Native Americans, Chinese Americans, and African Americans. During this time frame, the United States was expanding westward, the Civil War united north and south, and the greatest immigration wave was taking place at the turn of the century, and so America's identity was being formed and solidified. Thus the major focus was on socializing these students, and the teaching of the "three Rs" was secondary. In stage two (1954–1990s), the primary intent of schools was to instruct Mexican American students and to overcome the unequal and segregated schooling. However, stage two was founded on a deficit or disadvantaged premise. Under this view, teacher expectations were low because students were coming from impoverished communities, or a "culture of poverty." Additional federal funds and new programs were classified as compensatory in that they added resources to inadequate local school budgets. However, while there was some improvement, neither the additional federal dollars were sufficient nor the supplementary educational programs adequate. Stage three is currently in place (1990–present). It is under the blanket called "school reform." The school reform movement is driven by the political will of conservative publicly elected officials for accountability of taxpayers' money. The accountability perspective has been translated into raising standards for high school graduation, which in turn has produced high-stakes testing, first starting at the high school level, then moving to middle and elementary grade levels. Again, while the accountability movement has produced some positive results—mostly for white middle-class student bodies—it has done very little for students of color. For the most part the accountability approach has been just as detrimental to Latino students as the two previous eras of deficit thinking and Americanization. Higher standards and standardized testing have not reduced the dropout rates or reduced the achievement gap or increased high school graduation rates (Center on Education Policy, 2005). In fact, the increased high school graduation requirements and the statewide testing to measure the meeting of these higher standards are contributing to and sustaining these unwanted results, except for students of color who attend schools in middle-income communities (Nichols & Berliner, 2005).

Stage four is just now beginning to emerge, but only in very isolated cases. The federal initiative NCLB is for the most part carrying on a counterproductive approach like the previous movements. However, the one promising factor is its core belief that it will not accept any excuse from the public school community for students not achieving grade-level learning. From this fundamental tenet spring some other valuable elements. NCLB argues for highly qualified teachers, teachers holding high expectations for student success, periodic measurement of student progress, and disaggregating results by various student types. Also, NCLB shifts the burden slightly from the students to the schools. Before NCLB, the blame for poor performance was on the students because of their deficiencies, inadequate parental involvement, and poor community conditions. Or in short, the victim was blamed. NCLB now puts the onus on the school. But NCLB's continued use of the old labeling technique, only now applied to schools instead of students (underperforming schools, failing schools), produces resentment and resistance by school district personnel. Teachers and administrators are sensing what minority students and parents feel like when the "cause/blame" is placed upon them for nonsuccess in school. Consequently, educators react to their schools being negatively labeled by stating the difficulties they are saddled with: insufficient funds, too many federal mandates, restrictive procedures, factors beyond their control, and so forth.

By building on the positive tenets of NCLB and backed by its force of law,[1] stage four will flourish, as it has already in a few places across the country, and will sustain these recent efforts and spawn even more. What should stage four be? It must be centered on rethinking and redefinition so as to create sound and healthy new community schools. The three enabling factors are expanded on in the following sections.

BUILDING CAPACITY THROUGH STAFF DEVELOPMENT

It is generally accepted by college faculty and practitioners that preparation programs for teachers and other school staff (school building administrators and counselors) are not adequate for persons entering and serving in schools with high concentrations of students of color, such as Latinos of Mexican descent. College preparatory programs are inadequate partly due to lack of time (usually one year in length), faculty and curriculum with insufficient knowledge of such students, and lack of exposure and access to schools serving Latino communities. Therefore, most "real" learning occurs while on the job, and typically such learning is unsupervised, idiosyncratic, and haphazard due to its trial-and-error nature. Furthermore, most teaching staff within these schools have a fair-sized cadre of neophyte teachers at the start of each school year and high teacher turnover (because after gaining two or three years of teaching experience, teachers often move to school districts with higher pay scales).

Consequently, additional professional development of teachers and others is a must. As has been stated before in previous chapters, teaching and learning is a human enterprise. NCLB points out the need to have highly trained teachers if student learning is to be optimized. Thus district administrators in conjunction with the school building principal should put in place a targeted and continuous in-service training program. The topics should be focused, related to need, and connected to each other. In-service training should occur on a regular and frequent basis, at the school or in the community, and be led by persons who are rich in knowledge about the particular topic. To ensure cohesion, the in-service program should be planned for the entire school year before the school year begins. Also, to guarantee relevancy, the principal should chair a committee composed of school and community representatives. At various times in the development of the yearly in-service program, the committee should seek the feedback of the entire school.

What are some of the items that a Mexican American school-based staff development program should attend to on a regular basis? There are at least six umbrella areas: (1) utilizing language and culture in curriculum and instruction, (2) aligning classroom environment and practice, (3) living a set of student values, (4) creating a community service school, (5) managing organizational flux, and (6) building relationships, ad hoc and long term. These six targeted areas are broad in scope and thus will require multiple sessions in order to substantially cover them, not to mention to provide in-depth knowledge. The obvious must be stated here. By gaining knowledge about these areas, the school is building competency, or the ability to use the knowledge in a skillful way. Sessions should be designed so information is presented and discussed, and participants are required to simulate the competency or, at minimal, demonstrate it as it would be practiced. In so doing, the in-service training will model the student-centered concept being proposed for new Latino schools. The incorporation of community persons into the planning and operation of the staff development program will also translate back into the community.

It should be no surprise to the reader that language and culture are ranked as the number one areas for serious and continuous in-service training. If Latino schools for students of Mexican descent are to mirror their home and neighborhood life, then the Spanish language and the Mexican culture will have to be spoken and their heritage seen throughout the school. Traditional schools in Latino neighborhoods and communities will no longer be foreign territory. All school personnel will obviously need to undergo intensive language learning. At minimum, conversational Spanish must be known and practiced by teachers, administrators, counselors, and others throughout the school. However, the goal should be fluency and command of speaking, reading, and writing in Spanish. A side benefit of having school personnel learn Spanish is seeing firsthand what English language learners (students) face when they go to English-only schools.

Along with speaking the Spanish language, schools will need to reflect the blend of American and Mexican culture. Just as America is represented in schools through the holidays observed (e.g., the Fourth of July), foods dispensed in cafeterias, artwork displayed, and music played, so too should Mexican culture be made apparent in a parallel way (e.g., Cinco de Mayo). This means that all school staff, but in particular teachers, will need to know about Mexico's history, customs, food, art, music, and cultural icons, such as TV and movie stars, politicians, and sports figures. By gaining such knowledge, teachers and staff will come to have a greater appreciation for persons of Mexican ancestry, not only to reach students for teaching purposes but also to interact with students and parents on a personal basis. School personnel derive many benefits from learning a new language and knowing about Mexico. They will be bilingual and bicultural and so much more at ease engaging with parents and walking through neighborhoods. They will be secure in involving Spanish-speaking small-business persons. Being comfortable in the language and customs will motivate staff to travel on their vacations to different places in Mexico. And of course, by so doing, they will develop even more as global citizens.

The third reason for learning the Spanish language and Mexican culture is to infuse the Spanish language into classroom instruction and to incorporate the many elements of Mexican culture into the curriculum, particularly in the teaching of U.S. history. As a brief illustration, Spanish conquistadors were exploring North America from Mexico throughout the southwest and as far east as the Mississippi River (what are now the states of Arizona, California, Colorado, Florida, Louisiana, New Mexico, and Texas) before British colonists settled on the eastern coast of America; Mexican settlements were established in the southwest at the same time as the first permanent British settlements were being founded on the east coast of America (Santa Fe, 1608, and Jamestown, 1607); the immigration movement spread north from Mexico at the turn of the 20th century; and World War II prompted the *bracero* program.

Classroom environment is created from its organization (rules and ways of doing things) and teacher behavior (interaction with students). It is within a classroom structure that the majority of school time is spent by students and teachers. What happens and how it takes place here determine not only the amount of formal learning that occurs but also result in individual human development. Many Latino educators (Garcia & Guerra, 2003) have proposed that there is a mismatch between traditional classroom organization and Latino cultural norms. Hence, multiple staff development sessions must take place over an extended time period to examine what has been termed cultural discrimination by sociologists (Kendall, 1997). The purpose of these in-service sessions is to help teachers align their classrooms to be consistent with the Latino students' cultural and family upbringing. As with the other five umbrella areas for staff development coverage, there are too many to mention all. But for the sake of understanding and clarity, a few are mentioned herein.

First and foremost, the realignment within the classroom that should be explored and emphasized most is cooperative learning versus competitive learning. In the Mexican family, working to help each other so the family unit is made strong and protected from harm is a given. At the end of the day, fathers will ask the oldest son, "Did you help your younger brothers do their home tasks?" Daughters are expected to help with the household jobs, from caring for younger siblings to washing dishes. The emphasis is not "did you fulfill your particular responsibilities" but instead "did you help others." As we all know, U.S. classrooms are organized for individual learning, and success is measured through competition; the highest score is the best grade in class, and the best-behaved student gets the gold star. Also for the most part, schools minimize having better performing students tutor lesser performing students. Yet in the Mexican culture, older brothers and sisters are expected to not only help but also show younger siblings how to do a task correctly. By downplaying or, worse, removing this natural family approach in the classroom, it denies Latino students the opportunity to gain in stature in the eyes of others, build self-esteem and confidence, and feel successful. By incorporating group learning more, teachers will benefit by having more resources at their disposal —students helping students. We should also remember the construct that persons learn even as they take on the role of teacher.

In Mexican families, approval and feelings of worth are represented by touch. *Un abrazo* (a hug) between older males (e.g., brothers who are now fathers, cousins), between mothers with daughters, and so on is very common. Personal space between two people in the Mexican culture reveals acceptance, and the closer the better. Awarding gold stars at the elementary level to recognize good conduct or prizes at the secondary level is of little incentive. Furthermore, by keeping their distance from students (as teachers are taught in their preparation programs), they are inadvertently signaling minimal acceptance or approval of the students. Unfortunately, with more parental complaints to school boards about teachers touching students inappropriately and newspaper stories about criminal charges being filed with local police in isolated cases where a teacher was having an inappropriate relationship with a student, teachers are reminded not to touch students, no matter how innocent the pat on the head or the age of the child.

Since teacher behavior has been introduced, another commonly misdirected teacher behavior must be discussed. Classroom discipline is of major import throughout the class day and school year. Disciplining Latino students of Mexican descent is different from what has been taught in college programs. Typically, in teacher preparation programs, prospective teachers are told to have the student look them in the eyes to make sure the student is getting the message and then to ask the student to repeat what will happen if he or she breaks the rule again. In the Mexican culture, when a parent (typically the father) speaks to the son or daughter, the child naturally knows not to look the parent in the eye. The child must show respect and obedience in posture and not by words. A word of caution: It is not being proposed that all Mexican families operate like this example. However, the important point here is that school personnel need to find out for themselves how the Mexican home culture manifests itself with students at their school.

The third strand for in-service training is for teachers and administrators to operate from a new set of values: value students, value families, value change, value multiplicity, and value devotion by teachers. In this sense, *value* means to demonstrate worth and recognize contribution. For far too long, Latino students and parents have been devalued for who they are, for what they don't have, and for their lack of contribution or absence of support. After reading this far in the text, the reader will come to believe that the past view of Mexican students, families, and communities has been misrepresented, misunderstood, and consequently wrongly judged. By taking an opposite and positive view, the school as well as the students and parents will benefit. Instead of being depressed from lack of parental support and student cooperation, school personnel will be energized. Tension and distance will be replaced with good feelings and assistance. The next two values are change and multiplicity. At the end of the 20th century and the start of the 21st century, the belief that "the only real constant is change" has been frequently reiterated. With new ways of doing things and making products, the business world keeps changing. As technology moves forward, society changes. This societal change cannot be rejected or resisted in schools. Successful schools of the future will need to be flexible. So we need in-service training on two types of change: how to cope with an ever-changing environment and how best to incorporate changes that will make a positive difference in schools. Connected to the change element is multiplicity. There are multiple products to do the same thing, and no one size fits all, so teachers must learn to use multiple methods of teaching and various sources of curricula.

Finally, teacher dedication must be valued. Just as it has been proposed that we find new and better ways to interact with Latino students, parents, and communities, so too must we find ways to reinforce and support teachers who are devoted to helping students learn to their fullest. For too long the spiritual side of teachers, the mental hygiene of school administrators, and the psychological dimension of counselors have been neglected. What this book is proposing is a great load for school personnel. What the country's political leadership has been demanding is overwhelming, if not daunting given the lack of resources. Schools who are addressing this major challenge to create new community schools for Latino populations will need to honor, recognize, and appreciate the tremendous effort involved and the large amount of dedication required. The school community will need to close ranks and do this for themselves. At every opportunity available, teacher and administrator dedication should be acknowledged. The general public will not, the politician will not, the business community will not, at least at the beginning, value such dedication. However, as these islands of success are started and local communities are drawn in to provide assistance, then praise and recognition will be forthcoming from all these sectors mentioned. One recurrent occasion when teachers can be honored and reinforced for their dedication is at staff development training sessions.

Another umbrella area to be covered in staff development is outreach to parents and the rest of the community. More and more schools across the country are adopting the term *community school* in their formal names. By so doing, administrators are embracing the concept that schools are there to serve not just students but also the community. Clearly, schools should include parents in many ways and at a variety of times. Due to space limitations, only one "nontraditional" staff development way to encourage and conduct school outreach will be mentioned. Districts in low-income communities are dependent on every dollar they can get from the state. Most state dollars to schools are tied to ADA (average daily attendance). The entire school staff should select two or three days to walk the neighborhoods they serve in small groups of two or three, going door to door to remind parents when school starts. This simple event of teachers, administrators, and counselors walking in and through the neighborhood en masse provides psychological security to teachers who would fear to go out by themselves. It permits school personnel to meet parents in person, view home conditions, and begin to break down stereotypes. These walks demonstrate to parents and the community leaders that the school is concerned about the education of their children and is a community agency, a part of the local community. Last, by simply walking the community at the beginning of the school year (and following up two or three times during the school year), it is likely that more students will go to classes the first day of school. Hence teachers will have more instruction time with the students, students will start the school year well by participating in the orientation session, and the school will get its full share of state funding.

As previously mentioned, in-service training for managing organizational flux falls under the value of change and multiplicity. This change is on a larger scale. Valuing change was reviewed at a classroom level, but managing organizational flux is at the entire school level. While the responsibility for managing the school rests traditionally on the administrative staff, the literature on school change underscores the necessity of teachers and others being involved at all stages. Simply put, there must be "buy-in" by all. Everyone must be a stakeholder. Examples of schoolwide involvement include team teaching among the teachers at each grade level (for elementary schools) and "in-house" organization by grade level (for high schools). Another example of school reorganization is differentiated instruction. These restructuring approaches are offered because the intent is to get instructional staff to think how they can maximize their intellectual talent and organize their work time to create greater learning.

The last umbrella area offered for serious consideration for staff readiness is relationship building. Since it is being postulated that effective community schools will require new design and transformation, relationships and roles will have to follow suit. Regarding relationships, school personnel will need to know how to make connections with each other and externally with the many noneducation sectors. As we all know, working with external sectors is not natural for teachers and administrators. Identifying appropriate people from the outside of the school arena is not as simple as it looks. Determining the right approach when making contact (first impressions are important) along with ways to cultivate the contact over time is not always easy. Even within the school, relationship building will be new since we are no longer asking teachers to be isolated in the classroom but to work with each other on curriculum, students, extracurricular activities, and more.

With regard to roles, suffice it to say we are asking administrators to be managers, instructional supervisors, and community leaders; we are asking teachers to be team members and, even more, facilitators of student learning instead of playing the traditional role of the expert of all knowledge and center of the classroom. We will speak more to the changing role of teachers in the classroom in the next section on technology.

In summary, all the umbrella areas for staff development are targeted to enhance understanding of cultural diversity, expand the human resource, and turn schools into community service agencies.

USING AND INCORPORATING TECHNOLOGY

We all have heard that small class size, individualized instruction, abundant resources, teacher aids, strong parental involvement, and community support are some of the answers to fixing schools so that the majority of students achieve at grade level and even exceed expectations. But this is the ideal, not the reality. Schools in low-income communities have far less of a chance of acquiring high status. However, with the advent of technology and computers in schools heavily populated by Latinos, more can get done, done differently, and done better. How? By utilizing electronic learning as another methodology of teaching and learning, specifically to increase the practices of (1) diagnostic assessment, (2) continual monitoring of progress, and (3) developing tailored lesson plans for many more students.

Before discussing the utility of computers as a teaching and learning tool, the accessibility of technology should be pointed out. In 1996, the federal government began to provide assistance to schools acquiring computers and access to the Internet via the Telecommunications Act. When the program began, only 3% of the nation's classrooms were connected to the Internet. By 2005, after $14.6 billion in telecommunications discounts, more than 95%, or 91,000 schools, were wired (National School Board Association, 2005a). Because poor schools still lag behind in their technology, even after access to E-rate federal funds, they should continue to apply for more E-rate funds. Later in this chapter, another means of enhancing the school with technological tools will be shared.

During the 1960s, individualized instruction was being promoted and attempted. While it had much inherent conceptual value, in practice it was not feasible in most schools, particularly in poor schools. Individualized instruction required continuous data collection, analysis of student test results, multiple lesson plans, and different levels of instructional material. For elementary teachers with 30 or more students, with limited English-speaking skills and varying backgrounds, recent immigrant arrivals, and first-generation born Americans of Mexican descent, it was just too overwhelming. For secondary school teachers who had five class periods made up of 25 students or more (each class at different grade levels and different subject-matter focus), it also was declared impractical. However, the elements of individualized instruction are feasible. School districts now have on staff personnel who are specialists in designing programs to collect information about students in district schools. This is necessary in order to comply with the NCLB testing requirements. Districtwide student test-result data is not being used for diagnostic purposes; instead scores are now just for reporting numerical results. The next step is for school principals and teachers to request that a similar system be put in place at the school. More discussion on the point of data collection and its use for instructional and learning purposes will take place in chapter 7. The incorporation of computers, program software, and the Internet into classroom use is another ongoing staff development strand.

Computers and the Internet offer students a much richer learning environment. Computer software allows students to pace themselves according to their level of understanding. Programs allow for branching—if the response to a question is incorrect, the program will take the student through another route. Responses to questions are recorded, stored, and made available for the teacher to examine. The Internet provides access to a more stimulating set of materials, not just the printed word but also pictures, sounds, and motions. More assets of technology can be described, but instead it is important to stress the significant implication of the heightened use of technology in schools. First, as expressed before, the classroom teacher's role will need to change from one of expert, with all eyes on the teacher, to one of facilitator, where the teacher directs students how to find information on the computer. Second, schools will need to have two or more persons on staff who are technology experts. These employees provide support not just in the typical way of aiding teachers when they run into technological difficulty but also by being part of the team and acting as advisers on lesson plans for entire grade levels.

Last, school districts should contemplate replacing textbooks with laptops. Laptop computers could be assigned to students instead of textbooks on a semesterwide basis. By having laptops, students would have access to the Internet by day and could use their computers for work assignments at home. Schools should have learning labs with high-grade wireless computers that teachers can take into the classroom for certain group lessons and individual follow-up. The lab should be available to students and parents after school hours and during the weekend, much like the local public library.

FORGING MORE PARTNERSHIPS

So far in this chapter the classroom and teacher have been stressed. In this section, emphasis is placed on the district and school leadership. There are two very important functions that leaders must provide to employees in formal organizations. One is intangible; the other is materialistic. First, the invisible factor. School administrators must come to understand that current times and circumstances call for them to be leaders. Because the school communities have been under attack from various sources and find themselves in troubled times, educators need leaders who will create places that are not just secure but, now more than ever, where they can be creative and have space to maneuver as well. When change is necessary and in demand, then persons as individuals and as groups need to feel safe to be flexible, act in ways different from the norm, explore new avenues, work in different ways, relate to their colleagues and community persons in different ways, and learn from mistakes. Too often, in tough times, the norm is to restrict behavior and highlight the negative. Administrators who encourage excellence and renewal must become leaders who foster trust, emphasize thinking and examination, engender efficacy, and release energy—an attitude akin to John F. Kennedy's new frontier policies and the era of Camelot.

The other primary responsibility of the district superintendent and building principal is to bring to bear the necessary resources so teachers and students can be successful. It has been stated that teachers should assume a new role—that of being facilitators of learning. School administrators will need to be proactive instead of being managers. In business parlance, they will need to be entrepreneurs. Why? Besides bringing in more resources, they will need to think about how to downsize classroom numbers and to offer more services to community members so as to be full-service facilities.

It is clear Latino communities, as well as many other communities with similar profiles (mainly low income), cannot mount sufficient resources alone to put them in a position to create a more vibrant environment. There are a number of organizational features they can implement to strengthen their position and feasibility. One is to work closely with other like agencies or become, in organizational theory terms, tightly coupled (Weick, 1976). By this means, elementary schools connect their work with middle schools, and middle schools work seamlessly with high schools. Beyond a unified K–12 operation, a formal relationship is built with the community colleges, and the link is extended into the four-year colleges and universities. What Harold Hodgekinson (1999) called the "all one system" is now known as

K–16 compacts. In the beginning such work will require more committee meeting time, which few people are attracted to, but once the newness is worked out, many benefits are derived. Among the best are understanding what is happening before and after the student reaches and leaves the school (as well as reasons why); closing the "links in the pipeline" so students don't drop out; and knowing what to emphasize, thus saving much-needed time and energy. There are a number of associations that can act as resources to local communities that may want to start K–16 compacts; among them is Education Trust, headquartered in Washington, DC. In addition to establishing the traditional K–16 councils, it is proposed that parents and community members be included in the compacts as well. Another resource is the National Network of Partnership Schools, which released its eighth annual report of ways to involve families and the community in children's education. Eighty-six practices are listed that describe the best ways to sharpen purpose, add human energy, be more family friendly, and embrace children more positively (NNPS, 2005).

Another avenue for schools is to bring added resources by partnering with businesses. It was mentioned in chapter 2 how business partnerships could be helpful from an organizational restructuring perspective. The economic and human resource benefits are obvious, so they will be mentioned briefly. Economically, schools are encouraged to partner with computer giants such as Dell for donation of computers or restoration of computers. Partnering with national and local corporations to recruit their employees to become volunteer mentors to students and teachers is an added human resource for the school.

A third major sector to tap are national and local foundations. Many national foundations are interested in advancing the educational reform movement. One new player is the Bill and Melinda Gates Foundation (see chapter 9 for contact information). The most recent focus of the Gates Foundation is high school reform and helping minority youngsters to enter and complete college by providing scholarship support. The Gates' agenda and the rethinking of Latino schools are self-evident.

Finally, the federal government continues to be a major source of additional funds. While I understand the trials brought on by bureaucracy, the Latino education issue is rising in concern. It should be noted that since President Clinton, there has been a presidential committee on the educational excellence for Latinos.[2]

CONCLUSION

This book is about creating a new mind-set for change. However, schools, like other social agencies, are very reluctant to change themselves. For this reason, the chapter begins with yet another argument calling for school transformation. For those who are convinced there is a need to travel a more promising road, schools will need to position themselves to do so. In order to traverse this new highway, schools must enhance their capacity, primarily by enhancing their staff and creating an attitude that embraces change as a constant and empowers their staff to be flexible in coping with organizational flux.

NOTES

1. Formal resistance to NCLB is gaining enough momentum that it is likely to become ineffective. By September 2005, there were several pending lawsuits brought forth by local school districts and the NEA that challenged various aspects of NCLB. One of the challenged issues is the testing of non-English-speaking students in English. Also, several state legislatures are opposed to NCLB because the federal government is not providing adequate funding to states to underwrite the cost of implementing NCLB. As of this writing, resistance from local education agencies (LEAs), state legislatures, and teacher associations appears to be growing (see National School Board Association, 2005b).

2. In 1994, by Executive Order 12900, President Clinton created the President's Advisory Commission on Educational Excellence for Hispanic Americans. In 2001, President Bush continued this effort by establishing the White House Initiative on Educational Excellence for Hispanic Americans. A final report, "From Risk to Opportunity: Fulfilling the Educational Needs of Hispanic Americans in the 21st Century," was made available on April 9, 2002. The 18-month study represents a comprehensive plan to close the achievement gap for Hispanics.

Part III

HOTHOUSE ENVIRONMENTS, WELCOMING CAMPUSES, AND ENRICHING COMMUNITIES

In chapter 4, discussion was directed at the school district level, with focus on the prerequisites needed to start the metamorphosis (breaking away from the bureaucratic rigidity mold) of schools as well as to sustain the changeover on a yearly basis. In this part, chapter 5 will begin to narrow the focus of discussion of transformation at the school level, both elementary and secondary, and will continue to narrow the focus more in chapter 6, with emphasis on instruction and learning at the classroom level.

Chapter 5 uses a gardening analogy, specifically the use of the hothouse for growing, nurturing, and enriching the whole child, family, and community. The chapter goes beyond the narrow concern for greater student achievement and expands the school scope to include services to other critical players from the community. Schools will become welcoming cultural centers for the community that will concentrate on elements that are vital to the success of Latinos of Mexican descent. However, it should be acknowledged that much of what is written in chapter 5 and the book regarding effective education of Latinos is applicable to other students and communities of color in the United States, given their similar experiences and treatment.

Chapter 6 brings into sharper focus the longtime disconnect between the traditional Mexican culture and the school classroom. As a preview, most Mexican homes foster family and group identity, dependent on collective action to fulfill extended family responsibilities and human interaction for social entertainment, and facilitate learning via relationships among extended family members (e.g., storytelling by grandparents).

Currently, schools are overly regulated and exclusionary of low-income parents, and classrooms are organized for individual competition and isolated for a great part of the day. Chapter 6 discusses how classroom instruction should be organized to be compatible with Mexican home practices and values as well as what schools can do to be more in tune with the Latino community.

Again, suggestions are offered about how schools can manage more work by soliciting help and assistance from nontraditional sources. Furthermore, by the school and classroom mirroring the home structure, schools will be reorganized and will have fewer problems to distract them from their main task: growing, nurturing, and enriching the child, family, and community.

Chapter Five

Schools as True Places of Learning for Human Growth

In preparation for writing this chapter, I kept thinking of the saying "From a little acorn grows a mighty oak tree." The other phrase dancing in my mind was the title of the film *A Tree Grows in Brooklyn*. I mention both because these two titles represent what this book and chapter are aimed at. To elaborate, while trees grow easily in the country because of the favorable environment, it is not expected that trees grow as well in harsh urban conditions. Yet we find that in great metropolises such as New York, Boston, Chicago, and Los Angeles, many trees do grow and provide great beauty. These trees grow, not just in protected areas such as city parks but also along large boulevards, by busy streets, in shopping mall parking lots, and along major interstate highways within the central city. We know that a seedling will not take root, no matter how hardy or stout the stock, if it is buried under concrete and asphalt and subjected to harsh weather conditions. Yet gardeners have learned to grow trees in urban settings. It is not just a matter of transplanting young trees from a nursery; care and nurturing are required to help these trees mature. Because there are parallels between the care and nurturing of young trees and the care and nurturing of schoolchildren, we will use a gardening analogy throughout this chapter. In some places the matching points will be obvious. However, in a few places we will abandon the analogy for obvious reasons, specifically when discussion of bureaucracy begins.

THE WHOLE-PERSON APPROACH

The school being proposed must have a more ambitious goal than just being academically effective. It is not enough to say we want to close the historical achievement gap and bring all Latino students to grade level. Nor is it sufficient to say we want to have a 100% high school graduation rate. Neither should the goal be to have students complete public K–12 grades in order to be college acceptable. While all of these are fine outcomes, the true goal should be to have Latino youths be self-reliant and able to compete successfully in a global community—independent persons able to move into a future that continues to evolve and expand. With this broad mission as the stated target, it follows that schools must concern themselves with not just formally educating the student but also going beyond the traditional school scope to include experiences that take place outside the school and classroom walls. Schools should encompass the student as a whole person and the learning process as his or her human growth. With this enlarged mission, schools can no longer operate under the old paradigm. Now, skeptics might say I have gone overboard with this mission statement, that it is too grandiose. Not really. We must stretch the rubber band as far as we can in order to develop a new mind-set. Recall that it was President Kennedy who set the goal of travel to the moon, "not because it is easy but because it is hard." And the nation responded accordingly. We too in education can respond and be successful with this new challenge. Just as NASA had to be created to develop new technology to achieve Kennedy's goal, schools must be redefined. Educators should put on a new set of looking glasses to attend to this grand mission and goal for Latinos. Instead of continuing with the industrial and bureaucratic paradigms, a new paradigm that borrows from nature could be applied. Again I think adopting a different paradigm will serve to capture a new mind-set and provide us with a clear understanding of how to create such schools in a practical way.

Since we are now concerned with growing the child from a holistic perspective, learning life lessons can take place outside of school (after hours and on weekends). With this all-encompassing goal of holistic learning, families must be included; civic agencies (parks and recreation departments) and community-based organizations (who sponsor after-school and weekend programs) must be drawn into the learning process. With these new partnerships, more time and people are added to the educational process that do not come directly from the school. What is important is to have communication and collaboration with these external partners about what is taking place with each student, to match these nonschool learning experiences with classroom lessons as well as give credit and develop a fuller portfolio of each student's growth.

Casting a broader net of learning fits nicely with the gardening analogy. (Keep in mind that most soils will support growth; only the growing techniques differ.) Schools must reconnect and become a living part of the communities they are there to serve. They must see themselves as being planted in the community environs and as such will grow along with their students as a result of the added support they receive. In return, schools must give back to the community. By giving to and getting from each other, an ecological system develops that works together to achieve mutual benefits.

THE GARDENING ANALOGY

If we think of a garden nursery as the school district, the hothouse as the school, and pods within the hothouse as classrooms, it will be easier to understand what needs to be in place in new community schools for the following discussion. Also, the gardening analogy should help the reader think of more distinct comparisons than what is being offered. When we think of nurseries, we think of places where plants, grasses, flowers, and trees are raised into healthy and strong specimens.

How do nurseries grow robust and healthy plants? With apologies to horticulturalists, there are at least four rudimentary factors to the growth process. Stage one starts with the selection of the right ingredients (e.g., deciding on the proper soil mixture) and then moves on to the size and type of potting container. (Note that I am not including seed quality or "cuttings" at this stage. To do so would revert us to the old counterproductive argument that human genes, not schooling, determine educational outcome.) Stage two is constant and consistent inspection of the plants to note growth and color and to detect pests or onset of disease. Stage three is ongoing nutrition, including water and fertilizer. Stage four provides what I call balance, balance between the fundamental requirements of light, temperature, and moisture. If educators apply this simplified process when they design schools and operate instructionally in the classrooms, then we have to consider the following as comparisons. In stage one, determining the right starting ingredients, size of container would be number of students in the school and number of students in the classroom. Proper soil mixture would be the teacher's qualifications (at the secondary level, you wouldn't ask a music teacher to teach biology, or at the elementary level, you wouldn't place a non-Spanish-speaking teacher with students who speak only Spanish). In stage two, daily inspection, school personnel would want to establish a system where student growth and academic progress are monitored. In stage three, ongoing nutrition, educators would equate this to time allocation and instructional curricula. Finally in stage four, balance of the fundamental plant needs would involve the psychological aspect of motivation and technical follow-up. Let us develop each of these four stages further. But before doing so, please refer to Figure 5.1.

REQUIREMENTS

I.	II.	III.	IV.
Potting Ingredients	**Daily Inspection**	**Ongoing Nutrition**	**Balance of Fundamentals**
Soil composition, size of container	For growth, color, pests, disease	Water, fertilizer	Light, moisture, temperature

IN SCHOOLS/CLASSROOMS

I.	II.	III.	IV.
Rich Ingredients	**Daily Assessment**	**Adequate time**	**Psychological/ Technical**
Classroom size, instructional approach, volunteers, classroom aids	For progress or lack thereof, quizzes, homework	Lesson time, practice	Interaction, praise, correction motivation

FILL IN TEMPLATE FOR YOUR SCHOOL

I.	II.	III.	IV.
_____	_____	_____	_____
_____	_____	_____	_____

Figure 5.1. Template: The Hothouse for Full Growth and Development

After viewing the hothouse diagram, you will note that I have offered a few elements that fit into each stage. However, many other elements can be included, and for this reason I have left the lower part of the template empty for you to fill in. To further stimulate thinking and get the reader to understand how useful the gardening analogy is, I will sketch out just one or two essential elements within each of the four stages.

STAGE ONE: POTTING INGREDIENTS

In seeding, two critical elements are soil mixture and size of the pot to ensure germination. We know that school enrollment and class size matter. The larger the student number, the lesser the experience. The more students in a classroom, the less time teachers have to work with them on instructional matters and one-to-one instruction. Even worse, teachers have less ability to get to know their students as individuals and to develop a basic relationship of adult to youth. To forge a strong relationship between teacher and pupil requires understanding not just of the student's pattern of academic development but also of the home situation and family customs. Among the many theoretical constructs, educators know that learners are motivated when they can find meaning and usefulness in what is being taught. Many times, teachers have difficulty showing this direct connection in lessons, so they rely heavily on school rules and basic assumptions about the role of teacher and schools. That is, school is a place where students are required to attend, and while there, they are obligated to abide by the school rules and what the teacher tells them to do (i.e., don't challenge the teacher's or school's authority). However, if teachers take time to develop a relationship, students will come to accept what school authorities and teachers want them to do based on trust. If school personnel and teachers in particular take the time and effort to learn about students as people and as members of a family, children and parents will be more likely to trust the school and the teacher. They will come to believe that school personnel want to do what is best for the students. Also the more the teacher knows about a student and his or her family, the easier it is for the teacher to make connections between lessons learned and relevancy.

So to facilitate relationship building, teachers need to have smaller class enrollment size. How do we do this when these schools are typically overcrowded, understaffed, and underfunded? We do it by being creative, with the creativity coming from everyone throughout the school district. Governing boards will need to encourage school administrators to be flexible in staffing patterns through the passage of permissive policy. Boards will also have to help the superintendent to be more entrepreneurial in order to gain more human resource support. But at the school level, smaller units can be created even with larger student numbers. At the high school level, large high schools have been reorganized into "houses" by grade level. Each grade-level house is staffed with a house principal (instead of an assistant principal), counselors, and teachers. The house staff stays with the entering freshman class while they advance through the high school until graduation. By so doing, the house staff has four years to get to know the students. In addition, schools have "homerooms" where one teacher is assigned a group of students for the entire time they are at the high school. Over the four years, the homeroom teacher can and does develop a bonding relationship. There are other ways to develop relationships to get to know the student as a person and learner. An English teacher can be assigned a group of students from freshman to senior years, and these students take all their English course requirements from this same teacher. The same policy can be adopted for all the other academic subjects required, such as math, science, social studies, and so on.

What if the high school numbers are so great that the physical facilities cannot handle all the students at one time? Not the best of arrangements, but split-day sessions, where some portion of the students start later in the day, are an option. What else can be done? How about year-round schooling, not for the students but for the school. Again the same principle as the delayed daily schedule is followed, but now it is three months later for a cadre of students. But let's be even more creative. If we expand our concept of learning to take place outside of school, what about having students apprentice in the world of work for a certain amount of time? What about developing a service-learning curriculum that requires students to work on projects in the community? Under these two suggestions, students are away from the school facilities, but they are getting hands-on experience, guided by a mentor, someone in a community-based organization, someone in the business world, someone in the civic government or at the local hospital. This off-campus learning relieves the school staff from students as well, allowing them to work with fewer students.

Now the reader might say, these methods offered don't reduce class numbers. Remember the objective is not so much to lower class size as it is to develop a structure that will facilitate teachers to better attend to the students. Just as the gardener selects the right pot size and soil, he does so in order to manage and attend to the seedling. The gardener may start a seeding pod of 100 in the hothouse and another type of seeding pod of equal number, but he does so in a way that he can manage the necessary care. For example, he plants one pod one week and the second pod the following week so that later he can attend to them on alternate days.

What about the elementary school level? What can we do? Again, imagination is the main ingredient, and once more we offer what has been tried and found useful. The best way to lower the student–teacher ratio is to incorporate teacher aids and add resource teachers who take responsibility for students for a certain part of the day, thus releasing regular classroom teachers to do more with fewer kids. These aids can and should come from the community and parents, especially in schools with high Spanish-speaking learners. By utilizing and including aids as volunteers, particularly Spanish speakers, the school benefits in many ways. Teachers can learn Spanish from their aids on a functional basis, students learn content while learning English, school personnel learn about the Mexican culture, and teacher and aid (parent or community person) create an equal partnership, just to mention a few benefits.

To digress just slightly from how to lower the student–teacher ratio, but to be on point with the importance of redefining meaningful schools for Latinos, the value of speaking Spanish in school must be revisited. Why use the Spanish language for instruction and everyday school conversation? To communicate, to make sure the message is understood, and most important to build relationships and to bond with student and parents.

Antibilingual advocates, and those groups opposed to using Spanish in the classroom for instruction, say it is un-American, prevents students from learning English, delays their learning subject matter, and in the long run makes them less employable. However, studies with rigorous research designs reveal that it takes anywhere from two to three years to develop English language speaking and reading skills and three to five years to reach a level where students can compete academically in schools (Cummings, 1981). A similar study was undertaken by Collier, and equivalent findings were reported in 1987. A 2005 study, conducted by an Arizona State University colleague, Jeff MacSwan, showed that English language learners in Arizona who were forced by the public passage of Proposition 203 to learn English after only one school year of structured English language instruction had only a 29% gain in English proficiency; 71% experienced a zero or negative change in English proficiency (MacSwan, 2005). Think of the setback caused by such a negative experience, the loss of subject-matter learning, the psychological trauma suffered by these students, and the frustration felt by these teachers.

The reality is that parents want their children to learn English and, just as important, to learn reading, math, and science. Parents and their children understand that to be successful in the United States, they need to be proficient in English. Critics say that the longer Spanish speakers stay in bilingual programs, the less likely they will transition into English speakers. Nonsense! Very few people, much less low-income families and especially immigrants, want to work strenuous, labor-intensive jobs and earn low wages for the rest of their lives. They want a better life, especially for their children. Bilingual educators also want their students to be successful in school and in life.

People continue to come to America because it is the land of opportunity. They risk danger, even death, in crossing the border. But they want to achieve the American dream, and they are smart enough to know that learning English and obtaining a good education is the key to that success, both in the United States and the world. We are in a global economy with international trade. NAFTA (North American Free Trade Agreement), while struggling to reach its goal, is here to stay. American corporations understand that they need Spanish speakers and bicultural employees that fit well with Latin American businesses.

It was recommended in chapters 3 and 4 that schools use Spanish in the classroom because teachers need to communicate with their students in the language they understand in order to teach them subject matter from their very first day in school. Teachers cannot continue to lose valuable time by instructing in English when the child does not understand the language. Instruction in English only sets the wrong tone in the classroom; it can traumatize a student, making him or her feel dumb, uncomfortable, anxious, and nervous about school. Such feelings and teacher action do not make for starting a favorable relationship.

The immediate use of Spanish in the classroom is recommended so that students can understand the classroom expectations and rules, but more important so they can learn much-needed skills. This way both the teacher and student can start off positively and feel successful. Therefore, it is mandatory that Latino schools have a variety of language programs — ESL, bilingual education (both transitional and maintenance), and dual language. More will be written about these types of formal language instruction in chapter 6.

STAGE TWO: DAILY INSPECTION

In the gardening analogy, daily inspection of newly potted plants would be equivalent to a number of tasks undertaken at the school and classroom levels. I have selected to equate daily inspection to just one task, daily assessment of students in the classroom, or monitoring and reporting of student growth at the school level. When conducting regular inspection, the gardener looks for many things already listed in Figure 5.1, but with regard to trees, one particular aspect is straightness of the trunk. Is the tree growing without a major bend or slanted direction? As educators, we are taught in college at the onset of our teacher preparation programs that student assessment is vital for measuring teacher effectiveness in the instructional methodology used and student learning. Because of the heavy work press, classroom teachers reduce this important teaching tool of measuring student progress by giving short quizzes, assigning grades for homework assignments, or asking a few questions in class about the previous day's lesson. As a result, most teachers gain very little useful understanding of the students. To save time, quizzes are fill-in-the-blank type, and class questions solicit one- or two-word responses. I propose that teachers can collect useful information about each and every one of their students in an organic way, through teacher observation and conversation with students. Gardeners don't measure every one of their seedlings with rulers every day. They do inspect the rows and rows of pots while watering, weeding, and pruning. But more about this type of action is discussed in stage three. Teachers are being hammered to test more and get quantification-type data about student progress. This data collection in large part is due to the accountability

movement, which in turn is driven by the old "industrial model" thinking of public officials. More about the negative influence the industrial
paradigm produces will be shared after completing coverage of the four
stages in the gardening analogy. In previous chapters, I mentioned that
the role of the teacher should now be more of a facilitator than an instructor. In keeping with this notion, the teacher will collect more useful information from the student by setting up activities where the student, in cooperation with other students, practices what is being taught
in a lesson. During these student-centered learning activities, the teacher
should listen to what is being said, watch students performing tasks, and
converse with students. Placing emphasis on developing tests, adminis-
tering tests, collecting and grading tests, and then perhaps recording and
reporting letter grades or numerical scores takes time away from getting
to know students. This time is better used in ways suggested, actually
engaged with students via observation and conversation, both in and out
of class time. I need to caution the reader that I am not proposing to
eliminate all traditional testing and substitute it with classroom observation. Simply stated, teachers would be better served by doing more
firsthand observation rather than paper measurement or random classroom questioning of a few students.

What about the school level? Recall that the mission of the school
now should be the whole child coupled with the broader view that
students learn outside the school classroom and grounds. At the school
level, planning should occur with input from nonschool people. Parents
and representatives from community-based organizations, businesses,
and municipal agencies should be involved in discussions about
how students can and do learn outside the classroom. Field projects,
internships, work-study programs, mentoring programs, and reading
programs all should be considered and arranged. As part of these
learning events, feedback should be given to teachers so they gain a
fuller understanding of their students' growth and development. Certainly, in this time of computers and software programs, schools can de-
vise ways of collecting and tracking student activities and involvement
to share with teachers. The burden should not be on teachers alone. The
responsibility lies at the district and school levels. This link between
schools and the community will be discussed further at the end of the
chapter.

STAGE THREE: ONGOING NUTRITION

Stage three is simply referred to by the general public as the watering task. Of course it is more: There are times for providing plant food as well as determining the amount and time to provide water and what type of fertilizer. So when considering stage three in schools, educators can visualize an array of tasks. For the purpose of gaining understanding, I have selected the concept of time, or more precisely, determining the use of time in the classroom and at the school level, throughout the day and year.

In this era of technology where knowledge development and storage are growing exponentially, teachers are being pressed to pass on more subject matter (more historical facts and dates, reading, writing, science and math skills, and now technology) within a limited number of hours per day and a restricted number of semester days (typically about 178). At the same time, with an emphasis on accountability, schools are being pressured to be more effective in getting students to consume and digest all of this quantifiable stuff. And the stakes are higher; school report cards are now labeling schools as underperforming, failing, or excelling. Combining these two phenomena together, one gets the sense that schools and teachers are feeling they have less time to accomplish a greater workload, let alone practice in a new way. This whole scenario of raising standards and testing is the product of applying the industrial paradigm to schooling. To counteract these two clamps squeezing schools and low-income communities, it is proposed that schools take two actions. One is resist as much as possible the vice of "teaching to the test." Don't ignore the standards and the statewide test; instead come together as a district, as a school, and at grade level to examine the standards and dissect the state test to distill the essentials and prioritize what definitely needs to be taught. This first action, while probably considered to be mandatory given the tenure of the time, is not recommended as much as the second action. Under the new mission of caring for the whole child and serving the community, a broader definition of student learning comes into play. In fact it takes center stage. Schools should now be concerned primarily with character building (instilling the qualities of serving community, helping others, and becoming a civic leader) and raising a person to be a critical thinker, a decision maker, a contributor, and a successful competitor in an ever-evolving future. With this definition of student success, schools and teachers need to operate much differently than they have in the past. Picture in your mind alternative schools. These are the type of schools that have stripped themselves of bureaucracy and made themselves more meaningful to students and families. Think about the magnet schools developed because of court-ordered school desegregation and the storefront schools that emerged from the civil rights movement as two good examples. As educators, we must remind ourselves and the general public that education is a social process, not merely academic skill building. If we do not recall this important tenet (expressed best by John Dewey), then we will continue to be of disservice to all students and will not provide justice to Latino students.

Now let us connect this new definition of learning with the concept of time management. First, schools can manufacture more time: before and after school as well as on the weekends. Second, schools can get more persons involved as volunteers to tutor basic skills in reading, speaking, and writing. Third, schools can create a mentoring program and a speakers series where the mentors are role models with qualities the schools are trying to promote among the students, such as strong character. Potential speakers include community leaders, professionals, college students, and university graduates—Latino leaders with common backgrounds who come from similar communities. An excellent example is the newly elected mayor of Los Angeles, Antonio Villaraigosa.[1] Others can be city council members, congressional representatives, state legislators, county supervisors, corporate chief executive officers, or military officers.

STAGE FOUR: BALANCING THE FUNDAMENTALS

The last stage needed to grow healthy plants is that of maintaining a balance of fundamental elements. By now it should occur to the reader that the use of the term *stages* is a misnomer. Stages denote sequence, one followed by another, but what we are presenting and what actually happens in the hothouse is a process where all four stages take place concurrently and overlap at times—like what happens in the classroom with teaching. So the gardening analogy still fits very nicely. For this last stage in schools, I have identified the need for a good balance of psychological and technical additives. Too often, and particularly at the secondary level, there is an imbalance between these two elements. Similarly the early grades in elementary schools have an imbalance as well. Specifically, at the secondary level where middle and high school teachers are identified as subject-matter specialists (organized into departments), the emphasis is on cognitive development. In the early grades of the elementary level, the emphasis by teachers is on the affective domain, or acceptable behavior. In these new community schools for Latinos of Mexican origin, there must be a healthier balance between the two. Clearly, this is necessary if we are now concerned with the whole child, not just academic development but character development as well. Both the cognitive and affective will need to be attended to in a manner that best fits the student at the time. It needs to be noted that in the past, not only has there been an imbalance in these arenas, but also when one is stressed over the other, the attention has been skewed toward the negative side. Elementary teachers scold students for misbehavior in class less often than they praise good actions. Secondary teachers berate and embarrass students when they do poorly on a test or don't return homework instead of acknowledging satisfactory performance. The result is that Latino students form weak self-esteem. To get away from this destructive treatment (which teachers fall into unintentionally), I recommend that teachers and other school staff draw away from the pressure of testing for results and reengage with students in a holistic way, or on a person-to-person level. I recommend that school staff see themselves interacting with "little people" at the elementary level or teenagers at the secondary level, not limiting their view to these persons as math or biology students. By having a different filter to view youths, educators will contemplate their verbal interaction to be balanced and appropriate. That is, when attending to learning (cognitive domain), they provide technical assistance for correction or advancement. When teachers attend to the emotional side (affective domain), they praise to motivate the student instead of pointing out errors and unacceptable behavior.

With the previous discussion, it is hoped the reader can construct a new image of how schools need to evolve from caterpillar to butterfly. We now turn to discussing the hidden mental construct and the second major impediment to having good schooling for most students, but definitely for students of color and in particular Latino students.

MOVING AWAY FROM THE INDUSTRIAL MODEL

The emphasis has been to adopt a new mind-set, and to help with this task it has been proposed that educators turn toward a natural ecological paradigm. Educators have been fighting against the old industrial model paradigm, but elected officials and the business world keep using it when they try fixing the problems of the American educational system. That is to say, students are viewed as the "raw" product; schools are seen as the manufacturing plants where an assembly-line process is applied to students. Students are divided into grades and classrooms by age; curriculum is segregated into pieces by grade level; the teaching process is broken into so many days a year, lesson plans into so many minutes a day; and effectiveness is measured by testing students throughout the semester and at the end of the year. Elected officials and influential business persons use this industrial model to map their thinking, except when it comes to the input component. When educators remind these folks that cost matters, the response is that dollars are not all that critical. They quickly forget that when corporations plan for product improvement, the added cost of production is high on the agenda. (Not to mention that to maintain a quality product requires added cost, which is typically passed on to the customer in sales price.) As detrimental as the funding component is to education under the industrial model mind-set, it does not compare with the dysfunctionality of the whole model. Most regrettably, it does not appear that the nation will move away from this counterproductive mind-set. Therefore, to fight against this entrenched thinking and to try to capture this mode of thought to work in our favor, it is recommended that educators (particularly superintendents and principals) engage in forging new relationships. It is well known that schools where the majority of the student body is Latino are underfunded. Therefore, the leadership of these school districts and schools will need to concern themselves with developing a political constituency. Forging a political network leads to lobbying for greater influence at the local and state level. But capturing political support comes about if individuals are engaged with and represent a large group of people, in our case, the Mexican American community. Thus superintendents will have to bond with the needs of the district and the community. School principals will need to extend themselves to foster meaningful relationships with families and community leaders. These types of relationships transfer into social capital, which in turn may lead to unforeseen sponsorship and opportunities. Recall that with the ever-increasing population of Latinos across the country, politicians and corporate Americans are taking notice and trying to woo them. They know full well that large numbers translate into power.

Moving toward more community relationship building seems to have been occurring in big-city school districts in the past 10 years. Lately, more and more school districts in large metropolitan cities are coming under partial or total control of local city governments.[2] For example, in Boston, the mayor began appointing members to the school board in 1992. This movement should make it easier and logical to bring city services and aid into schools, as called for in this book. By moving the governance function under the umbrella of the mayor, city officials should understand firsthand the hardship that schools must deal with. This move should help to lobby for more funds from multiple sources (e.g., levying for a better tax structure and more tax dollars; getting a share of the city's budget allocated for parks and recreation and restricting these funds for school partnership programs; and helping to influence the state legislature for more funds).

MOVING TO FULL-SERVICE COMMUNITY SCHOOLS

For Latino schools to become effective in teaching the whole student, they will need to take on more responsibility than just educating the student on subject matter. They will need to expand the services provided to the community within the school's geographic boundary. This expansion will require additional resources, but a community-serving school will in return bring in additional human and financial resources. How? By extending itself, the school will be able to get more professional assistance and human support (e.g., volunteers to act as classroom aids and persons to assist others throughout the school) (Warren, 2005).

In keeping with the gardening analogy, I want to attach another related metaphor to extend the analogy just a bit further. As society advanced during the latter half of the 20th century, so did the operation of the grocery store. What began as the neighborhood, corner grocery store, owned and operated by mom and pop, who lived in the back of the store, was eventually superseded by the supermarket. Corner grocery stores at first sold only the essential foods (meats, vegetables, fruits, bread, and milk), then increased their stock to other necessities (household goods). Being within walking distance made them viable. Since customers and store owners were stable (few families moved away), stores were able to add some services later to stay competitive with the emerging chain market. These services included home delivery of orders made by phone and allowing customers to purchase goods on their credit accounts (store owners kept a large ledger at the pay counter, and the neighborhood customer carried a small notepad, where costs were recorded in pencil). However by the late 1950s, the corner grocery store was overcome by the supermarket. With autos becoming more affordable and suburbs developing, these supermarkets served a much larger geographic area. They had the capacity to shelve more brand-name products, stock a larger inventory, offer reduced prices, and offer other in-house services such as bakeries and flower shops. Currently, supermarkets are open 24 hours a day, seven days a week. Their services have grown to include pharmacies; banks and ATM machines; photo development; customer service booths where checks are cashed and money orders issued; and hardware, houseware, gardening, and electronics sections. Finally, these supermarkets are issuing electronic discount cards, which are used to track their customers. Customers can request home delivery of an order placed online, and they may look up sales on the store web page.

It is proposed that the new Latino school be a full-service community agent that patterns itself much like the supermarket of today. What specifically? The following should be provided: medical, legal, employment, and municipal services; instructional programs for parents and adults from the community; and a recreational/entertainment venue. Let's describe each one somewhat.

Medical and health services are critical. We all know students learn very little if they are hungry, are visually or hearing impaired, are mildly ill, suffer from allergies, or have dental problems. School nurses are not readily available on a full-time basis, due to financial shortfalls in school budgets. What is being proposed far exceeds a full-time (five days a week) school nurse. Eye examinations should be given to every student once a year, and dental checkups performed twice a year. Immunization against childhood diseases should be provided. Also, free goods should be given at the time services are rendered (e.g., at dental examinations, tooth-brushes, mouthwash, and dental floss should be provided; when students see a nurse or a doctor for an illness, they should get free over-the-counter medication, such as treatment for coughs, colds, and minor scrapes). But how to cover these additional services? Utilizing volunteer physicians and nurses from local hospitals and private practice, as well as medical students from nearby medical schools (of course, supervised by a certified nurse or doctor), is one approach.

Legal aid to parents and teenagers is another service that should be provided at the school. Information should be available about small claims disputes, traffic citations, dealing with auto or work accidents, immigration rights, handling threats about past-due bill payments, landlord/tenant disputes, eviction notices from absentee landlords, and so on. Again these services should come from volunteers. There are professional associations of Latino attorneys (in Phoenix, *Los Abogados*) who are typically willing to contribute pro bono time, and there are law students who are equally willing to give of their time.

Many parents want to learn English or improve their English skills. Schools should provide English language learning classes after school and on weekends. While there are many benefits gained from this service, the one main benefit is English-only teachers will be able to communicate with Spanish-only parents with much more ease of mind. Any school teacher who conducts these additional classes should be monetarily compensated by the district. Another instructional service should be a class on learning to pass the driver's license written test. It should be taught by a police officer, as community service. Last of all, continuing education should be provided, and some classes could be taught by skilled community volunteers. These short offerings could also be given by partnering with a local community college, where their instructors and students could volunteer as part of service-learning projects.

Municipal governments such as the city or county should be present on local campuses after school hours during workdays and weekends so residents have easy access (within walking distance) to pay bills, inquire about notices, get official forms, and obtain guidance in following procedures for paying local taxes.

Employment services should be considered. Such services should be updated regularly, with vacancies and referrals posted, as well as offer tips on getting hired, filling out applications, resume writing, and interviewing techniques. The postings could be for daily work, temporary work, and long-term employment. Labor union representatives could provide this type of service, and large employers could come on campus once a week for a few hours.

Cultural entertainment would be periodic and seasonal depending on artist availability to perform or display their crafts, whether music, dance, arts and crafts, films or theater. The school can be a venue to feature new local talent, such as new bands from the neighborhood who are trying to get started, and new artists can exhibit in school hallways.

By reaching out and providing services, the school will be in a better position to get volunteers to undertake these added responsibilities. In so doing, the community will be better prepared to give of themselves as well as wanting to contribute their time as aids in the school. In short, the school will get much more in return than what it has given.

The last item that schools can adopt from the supermarket model is the shoppers card. Recall that markets encourage their regular shoppers to register for their store card to receive store discounts. But these cards are also used to track the customer. This use of technology should be applied to students in schools. Smart cards should be issued to students and parents. Card-reading machines can be brought into schools (donated from companies, of course), and students and parents would "swipe" their cards for services used. For students, a software program could be set up to collect student data such as homework turned in, attendance at after-school events, tutoring sessions, and field trips attended.

CONCLUSION

The previous illustration of using credit card technology best captures our effort in this chapter. Specifically, teachers need to envision schools for Latinos in new ways. By expanding their mission to be holistic and full service, and by incorporating the community, educators can be enriched (not burdened) and become more effective in fulfilling their teaching responsibilities.

NOTES

1. Mayor Villaraigosa is a product of the prevailing schooling that is very much in need of an overhaul. As such, Villaraigosa, Texas congressman Ruben Hinojosa, and L.A. County supervisor Gloria Molina are the exception rather than the rule. The new community schools being proposed herein should develop many more leaders as the rule rather than the exception.

2. As of this writing, a growing number of state and local officials are complaining publicly that there is greater intrusion into local school governance by the federal government with all the mandates of No Child Left Behind. In Los Angeles, the mayor is attempting to have the school district under his control for the next six years.

Chapter Six

Organizing Schools for Latino Learners and Fostering Creativity

About two years before writing this book, at a retreat where the program faculty were contemplating the future of our preparation program, an alumnus (representing the students' views) asked me what I wanted the leadership preparation program to be. I quickly replied, "I want it to prepare future leaders so they can create high-stepping and fast-striding schools, where the music played [or the instruction and learning performed] is uplifting, imaginative, and syncopated!" This reply applies to this chapter. To create uplifting schools where creativity is the hallmark of everyone's work, five areas must be attended to: (1) building a strong sense of community within the school itself; (2) utilizing language throughout the school in a liberating way; (3) ensuring there are a variety of formal language instructional programs, not just one type; (4) making instruction and learning in the classroom atypical from the traditional methodology; and (5) ensuring instruction and learning outside of school is attended to not as extracurricular but as a necessary and integrated part of a student's school learning so as to be consistent with the holistic approach.

A STRONG SENSE OF SCHOOL COMMUNITY

Much has been said previously about establishing the right type of mind-set, or attitude, in our schools of the future. Because this mental construct is so vital to the remaking of schools, even more must be expressed. Unfortunately, due in large part to oversized enrollments, especially in high-growth communities, along with society's trend to saddle schools with added responsibilities to solve emerging problems, school personnel have been greatly pressured to concentrate on results; to spend less time on relevant curricula; and to spend more time on fulfilling school responsibilities such as sponsoring student clubs, covering school-yard duties, and working on and at athletic events. High-enrollment schools focused on outcomes and nonessential tasks have become impersonal places. The human dimension has been reduced to a small consideration. On top of all this, as is well known, teaching is an isolated profession because teachers work 90% of their time in a classroom that is closed off from others. When teachers and others do come together, it is generally in subunits of the school (e.g., grade-level teachers, counselors, or departmental meetings). The school meetings where all employees come together are typically infrequent, noninteractive, and focused on superficial agenda items. As such, most school staff do not know each other well, and depending on the size of the school and the annual mobility rate of teacher assignments (turnover), many schools are a reflection of today's suburbs (i.e., bedroom communities in name only since residents spend the majority of their time away from the house, and therefore few people know their neighbors).

In our new definition of schools, the human dimension is important and needs to be a priority. The Mexican culture values social engagement and gains enjoyment from human contact and simple conversation. Therefore, it is necessary for schools to think about developing into a true community, not just developing school spirit for athletics. By developing community within schools I mean stressing the human element of caring for one another, for students, for their families, for colleagues, and for other school support staff. By caring about others, we will want to instinctively do what is right or best for them. Putting people first becomes paramount. This single characteristic of caring is so important in education, in the school community, and in the classroom, and yet it has been elbowed out to a large degree from the act of teaching. Hopefully, with the newly formed Teacher Education Accreditation Council's inclusion of this quality in its mission statement and criteria for endorsing teacher preparation programs, it will return with greater force.[1] Caring comes primarily from the heart. When asked by a student in the audience during a TV interview on *Inside the Actors Studio* (2005) why she was so successful and so well connected with her audiences, Barbra Streisand replied, "What comes from the heart goes to the heart." In her work (stage performances, recordings, acting, and directing), Streisand humanizes rather than intellectualizes. She is in a people business and needs to connect on a personal and affective basis. So too education and teaching are human enterprises. If we are to reach persons, we must bond with them. Touching the minds of students is achieved through caring from the heart.

Caring is both a product and the outcome of togetherness and understanding that all parts of the school are connected and interrelated. How can educators forge a school community with caring as its cornerstone? A number of proven ways come to mind. Organizations promote togetherness or unity by agreeing to a set of common goals, by scheduling regular meetings of the whole, by having frequent and open (two-way) communication, and by working collaboratively instead of separately. These ways and means should translate easily into holding schoolwide meetings more often than just at the start and end of each semester. Handle these schoolwide meetings as town hall sessions, where communication is among the whole group not just a question-and-answer session, typically between the principal and those present. Also, when thinking about interrelatedness, remember to be inclusive and think of the larger community, beyond the school. Communication spans more than town hall meetings; it should come to mean dialogue and discussion in work groups, in team meetings, in planning sessions, in project evaluations, and so on.

Building community is necessary for schools to redo themselves. A recently published book (see Horowitz, 2005) examined high schools that were struggling to teach the so-called disadvantaged students. Among the many strategies the study found in schools that were able to turn their situation into one of achievement were (1) create a school climate of optimism and success for students and teachers; (2) partner with feeder middle schools, businesses, and colleges for long-term success; (3) hold students to high expectations; (4) coordinate lesson plans and tests within departments and across grade levels; and (5) develop flexible school systems to maintain reforms that work. These five school actions are identified here (out of a longer list) because they reinforce what should take place in redefining schools for effective Latino learning.

USE AND DEVELOPMENT OF LANGUAGE
THROUGHOUT THE SCHOOL

It was estimated that in 2004, just under five million English language learners (ELLs) were enrolled in public schools (National Center for Education Statistics, 2005). The exact total is not as important as the trend. It is projected that ELL student enrollment will double by the year 2020, whereas "regular" student enrollment will grow by only 22% (Kindler, 2002). This projected rate of growth for ELLs is probably on the conservative side. The ELL student growth could and probably will be greater than projected, due to the ever-increasing general migration from Mexico. A modern all-time high of 1.55 million foreign annual arrivals was reached in 2005. This total exceeded the 2004 yearly migration number of 1.22 million (Gibson & Rodriguez, 2005). Factor into this equation that Hispanic birthrates are higher than that of whites and that the average Latino population age is the youngest of all ethnic/racial groups, and it is easy to conclude that the future major enrollment wave in public schools will be Latino, particularly of Mexican ancestry, since Mexicans make up 60% of the total U.S. Latino population. This Latino student growth coupled with the per annual teacher shortage presents a major problem. Public schools are deficient when it comes to having Spanish-speaking teachers and administrators on their staff. Even worse, college teacher preparation programs across the country are not producing sufficient numbers of teachers to compensate for the general and overall student growth and projected teacher retirements. The ever-present teacher shortage is reaching a crisis stage in a number of important areas (e.g., bilingual teachers, special education, math, and science). So how can schools help themselves correct this sizable imbalance?

First, schools as a community must commit to the idea that knowing and using Spanish throughout the school is a plus and not a preexisting negative condition that must be overcome by parents and students alone. When school personnel realize they are part of the problem (for not knowing the Spanish language, the tongue of those they are to serve), then and only then will they become part of the real solution. Once they have adopted the belief that Spanish is useful, then strategies to build Spanish language capability and usage will surface. Here are a few suggestions that can help kick-start the usage of Spanish in the school.

Spanish is spoken in many if not all the Latino families the school serves and is spoken in the community by business persons and many others. Therefore these schools are rich in the Spanish language; they are surrounded by the use of the language, both orally and written. Consequently, they should tap into this asset. Schools should reach out to members in the community to teach conversational Spanish to all the staff. After developing conversational Spanish, teachers should learn how to read and write Spanish equivalent to what is taught at the high school level for students (i.e., Spanish I and II). This should not be difficult for college-educated graduates. School districts should also compensate teachers who develop their language ability. By doing so, schools can incorporate other community-based Spanish language resources (e.g., using the local Spanish language newspaper in classrooms). Most of the community newspapers are bilingual, with stories and advertisements written in both English and Spanish. As well, with the advent of national Spanish language television networks, such as Telemundo and Univison, teachers can tie learning assignments to news reports and local community-interest programming. Not all teachers will become Spanish language literate; some may stop at the conversational stage. What is important is that they make an effort to increase their capability to communicate with Spanish speakers and that the public see their effort. When I was collecting field-based ideas of how schools could close the achievement gap or increase Latino learning, a Chicano high school principal expressed the value of teacher effort so well when he said, "If a teacher finds it too difficult to have a bilingual tongue, parents must see that they tried and in so doing have a bilingual heart."[2]

The school should extend its role of language development outside the campus and into the community. That is, offer English classes to students who dropped out of school and to parents and grandparents who want to learn English or improve their English language skills. In turn, get these adults to read to their elementary children in Spanish. Have the children read to their parents and grandparents in English. The schools would be promoting learning at home and incorporating parents into the learning process, making students tutors and parents partners in the education process. This is the beginning of creating learning communities. The core value of this type of family inclusion in the teaching and learning process is the acceptance by teachers and the school of the concept of partnership.

Educators of color have written that schools, and teachers in particular, need to bond with communities and parents to learn the culture and forge strong relationships with families (Lawrence-Lightfoot, 1978). There is no better way to interact with each other than by learning each other's language.

By creating partnerships, some meaningful by-products are established. The relationship between teachers and parents shifts into one of parity. Both acknowledge they are deficient in the use of either Spanish or English. Both become instructors for each other, teachers learning Spanish from parents and parents learning English from teachers. Understanding and appreciation of the Mexican culture grows in stature within the school, and the American socialization process takes root in the Latino communities. A new identity emerges, a mixture of the Mexican and American. Through all the media outlets (TV, radio, music, films, and sports), we have seen and heard the changes in food, fashion, and language trends that reflect a Latin flavor. Equally, second- and third-generation Latinos of Mexican descent are forging identities that are much different from previous U.S. Latino-born generations.[3] Because of the intradiversity among Mexican Latinos, schools need to have a variety of language development programs. These programs should match student needs and community circumstances.

FORMAL PROGRAMS TO PROMOTE TWO LANGUAGES AMONG STUDENTS

The new community schools for Latinos will need to have at least one and preferably more than one language development program for students. Basically there are two main program designs: English as a second language, commonly called ESL, and bilingual education. Under the ESL approach, the teacher does not need to know a student's native language and can teach English language development to a classroom of students who speak different foreign languages. An ESL classroom might have Chinese, Spanish, French, German, and Russian speakers all mixed together. The primary ESL objective is to have non-English-speaking students learn English as quickly as possible so that they understand English spoken to them and can respond in kind. Students who are being taught in the ESL

mode are typically kept in a classroom unto themselves and are not assigned to a regular (English-speaking) classroom until they can converse
in English. Once inserted into a regular classroom, depending on the student's English proficiency, the student may be "pulled out" of his or her
regular class to spend some more time in an ESL classroom.

The goal of bilingual education is to make the student proficient in two
languages, his or her native language and of course English. Accordingly,
the teacher should be bilingual, literate in both English and the student's
native language. Also since language is inseparable from the culture it
represents, bilingual education includes the learning of the student's
homeland culture. Bilingual language development is consistent with the
tenet found in the teaching of any foreign language. It is learning not just
new vocabulary, pronunciation, sentence structure, or technical language
development but also about the country's culture, such as food, music,
holidays, history, geography, and customs. Behind this tenet is the logic
that language is best learned when it becomes relevant, or put into a context for functionality.

There are variations of each of these two basic approaches. With bilin-
gual/bicultural education, there are two main subtypes: transitional and
maintenance. The difference between the two is found in their respective
objective. The transitional approach aims to get the Spanish speaker (in
our case) to be proficient in English as quickly as possible. After exiting
the transitional program, English language development occurs naturally
(typically at home) and by means other than formal school instruction
(TV, radio, and newspapers). The maintenance bilingual program's target
is to continue to develop both English and Spanish concurrently. As such,
the student does not exit the bilingual program (Andersson & Boyer,
1970).

Proponents of bilingual/bicultural education evolved yet another form
of the maintenance program by creating dual-language instruction. Dual-
language schools are places where all students learn two languages: English and typically Spanish in the United States, English and French in
Canada. The value of a dual-language school is that it raises the status of
the second language (in our case, Spanish) so that it is equal to the country's first language (in the United States, English). That is, a person who
is able to communicate in two languages has an advantage over a person
who can speak only one language. It supports the long-held European

definition of an educated person as one who can communicate in more than one language. The dual-language school was also created to counteract the stigma that students in bilingual programs faced. Since bilingual educational programs of the 1960s were promoted to compensate for the poor instruction that limited-English-speaking students were receiving, and since they were placed under the umbrella of federal compensatory programs, bilingual education quickly became labeled as remedial and identified with immigrants and poor students. Under the dual-language school design, English-speaking students from middle-income communities who spoke only English would now benefit from learning a second language (Spanish) while concurrently being taught in English.[4] The latest evolution of dual-language schools is a two-way approach. Whereas in the dual-language approach the classroom teacher is bilingual, in two-way schools, a teacher can be primarily monolingual in English and the school has a few teachers that are proficient in Spanish. In this situation, Spanish-proficient teachers enter the classroom to teach in Spanish for half of the time.

Given the brief description of the programs devised to upgrade English language skills of non-English-speaking or LEP students, it should occur to the reader that a bilingual/bicultural education program be implemented in these new schools at minimum and at best the dual-language approach be put in place. However, knowing that schools are at different stages of readiness and communities are also at different phases of political acceptance, I underscore the recommendation offered by the National Research Council. The key is not finding one program type that works at every school for all students but designing a program based on student needs and community resources (August & Hakuta, 1998).

CLASSROOM INSTRUCTION AND LEARNING

Within the classroom, two basic functions take place: teaching and learning. Instruction, provided by the teacher, is intended to lead to student learning. The more effective the instruction, supposedly the more the students learn. However, it must be cautioned that this is not a one-to-one correlation. For purpose of emphasis, I have divided instruction into two parts, mental and operational. The learning part is divided into four elements.

Let us begin with the mental, or thinking, part of instruction. First and foremost, teachers must have high expectations about their students' academic achievement. They need to believe strongly that their students have more than a satisfactory capability for learning. In addition, teachers must come to believe that they can teach any child to learn. That is, no excuses are allowed, or as I would say to education majors during their first-year orientation, "No student is expendable." Teacher expectation and its impact on student learning is well researched.[5] No more needs to be said, except to state that this positive teacher attitude must be in place in Latino schools as bedrock. Next, teachers must stress teaching that fosters creative thinking by their students. While educators declare that they are dedicated to preparing students to be critical thinkers, schools are organized, at least for low-income communities, to generate routine and regimentation. Stress is shown by the use of such phrases as "respect authority," "don't question," or "do as you are told." How can teachers promote creativity? One example is in writing. Instead of underscoring the technical aspects of writing (proper grammar, spelling, capitalization, punctuation, and so on), have students write to express themselves on paper. Ask them to write about a story they have heard or their reaction to a movie or TV program, about a member of their family, or about any personal experience. Students should not concern themselves with any of the mechanics; just get them to express themselves. Once they feel comfortable with writing, take them to the next level of creative writing by having them imagine and make up stories. One way to stimulate the imagination is to invite their parents, or better yet their grandparents, to come to school and tell stories that have been passed down orally from one generation to the next. As part of these storytelling events, have students write about their reactions. After this creative writing phase is well advanced, teachers can attend to the basic technical aspects, but not too much or too quickly or you defeat the purpose (i.e., students can develop writer's block). The National Association of Secondary School Principals (2005) produced a guide for middle and high school principals that provides practical steps and examples of ways to confront the deficit in literacy skills. It is titled *Creating a Culture of Literacy*.

Along with advancing creative thinking and writing, push for the elimination of the math phobia. There is a general misconception that mathematics in particular and sciences in general involve lockstep deductive reasoning skills too abstract to understand. However, the National Council of Teachers of Mathematics has made great strides in reducing math phobia among teachers and students. Among the many math professors working to reverse the mental fear of math is Edward B. Burger. He, like many others, prefers teaching math in a creative storytelling fashion.[6] (See the reference section for his new book, coauthored with Michael Starbird.)

Moving along to the practice of teaching in the classroom, let me emphasize that these practices should be part of the teaching styles in these new schools. Teachers should be organized into teams to facilitate their working together on a daily basis to plan short- and long-range lessons, activate team teaching and differentiated instruction, and assess both student learning and lesson implementation. Teams should be formed at the secondary level across subject matter and at the elementary level across grades. By so doing, a number of pitfalls are eliminated. For example, teachers get to know the child as a whole student, not just by how well he or she does in history or English or science. A student may not do well in one subject area yet excel in another. In cross-disciplinary teams, teachers can gain insight as to how to help students learn subject matter they are struggling with by observing them in sessions in which they do well. Also, teachers in teams can see themselves as being a speech teacher or a writing teacher since these two skills are needed in all classrooms, no matter the subject area. In short, teaching teams can practice writing across the curriculum with more cohesiveness.

Additionally, team teaching allows for more flexibility in the utilization of instructional time during the school day. By working cooperatively, teachers in teams can see the unevenness of their students' learning in certain objectives (i.e., curriculum standards that will be tested at the end of the school year) and as such can then differentiate the instructional time to match the need—more time on a certain objective and less time on another. Furthermore, teachers in teams have different strengths and weaknesses. Clearly, teams can match a teacher's strengths with student needs to maximize student learning.

Teachers must operate differently than in the past if Latino students are to learn more. Four actions must become repetitive: diagnosing, developing individual learning plans, assigning student-centered activities, and monitoring. One of the best instructional/measurement tools has become a double-bladed weapon used against students (i.e., its sharp blade wounds instead of cutting to heal). Teachers test students far too often, and in so doing, students who do badly become demoralized and start believing and accepting less of themselves. To reverse this banal trend, it becomes imperative that teachers practice diagnosing students' learning habits. When diagnosing students, teachers are forced to discover what is happening and why. By probing beneath the surface (i.e., just scoring to record a letter grade or number of questions a student got wrong) and examining which questions were answered incorrectly and inquiring why (is there a pattern?), the teacher can design a follow-up activity that will help a student learn the objective. In short, the learning cycle begins by the teacher diagnosing the student. With this useful information, the teacher (team) can open a portfolio on each student and develop an ILP, individual learning plan. This tailored ILP approach is mandatory for all students in special education programs because a student so designated has a specific learning disability that requires particular attention. An ILP is an overview of a long-term comprehensive plan. For our purposes, an ILP for Latino students does not need to be as detailed as required for a special education student. As a former school practitioner, I realize that the special education circumstances are much different from the regular classroom, mainly student–teacher ratio in special education is much lower. However, developing individual student portfolios is now possible because of two factors: (1) the inclusion of technology (mainly computers and software programs) and (2) the organization of teachers into teams, with community volunteers who provide guided learning outside the school. (More will be said about out-of-school learning in the next section.) With information gained from diagnostic practice, and an overall plan started for each student, then teacher teams could develop lessons in which the student is in an active mode. The more a person is engaged in an activity, either mentally or physically, the more likely he or she will learn. What is being called for here is more than worksheets and drills under the rubric of practice and repetition. Discovery and study groups are being proposed. Last, in closing the learning cycle, teachers should end the way they started, by monitoring progress through assessment (i.e., collecting information about the student's learning through observing, listening, and questioning rather than just simple paper and pencil testing). The monitoring stage of this "do loop" starts the loop again. Once again, if no progress is shown, the student should not simply repeat the lesson in the same way in the hopes that he or she just needs more time and practice. Only by using the tool of diagnosing will the next step be validated.

OUT-OF-SCHOOL LEARNING

Throughout this book I have proposed that new schools serving Latino students must extend themselves to be full-service, community-centered institutions. Others have suggested that schools will benefit greatly in return for what appears to be a burdensome overextension. Hopefully by now the reader is convinced that the return exceeds the demands. But if not, here are four more persuasive arguments. It can be said that almost all parents value education. However, with much certainty, it is safe to say that Latino parents value education highly. They desperately want their children to go to school and get a good education. In the traditional Mexican culture, *maestras* (teachers) are respected members of society, receiving much more than the lip service given to teachers in the United States. Countless Latino dignitaries, successful public figures in entertainment and sports, when interviewed about their upbringing, will recall how their parents stressed the importance of doing well in school.[7] At a young age, Mexican American kids are admonished by their parents to mind the teacher, to work hard, and above all to do well in school.

Another argument for community schools may have more influence. As is well known, education has been under the public microscope since 1983 (see the U.S. Department of Education publication *A Nation at Risk*). This public scrutiny was heightened in the early 1990s with the accountability movement. At the turn of the 21st century, the target for change in public education became the high school. According to a survey result released by the Alliance for Excellent Education (2005), 83% of Americans believe that high schools are in urgent need of improvement. The same poll also showed that 79% of the public believe that middle schools need to improve, and 76% believe elementary schools are in need of improvement. Their need-for-change view is based on the low graduation rates and too few high school graduates having employable skills or being prepared to go to college. The public believes that better schools are needed, not just to produce better graduates but also to maintain a strong

U.S. society and keep the country as a leader in a global economy. Even more telling, the same survey results indicated that 94% of African Americans want school improvement, as do 82% of Hispanics. In short, schools have a large support base (more than 75% of all populations and more than 80% of persons of color). Schools should tap into this support for school improvement. Schools should tell Latino communities that they want to create better schools, but to do this they will require each community's help in many ways.

Add community-based organizations (CBOs) to this public support for improvement. CBOs emerged during the civil rights movement to empower minority communities by opening job-skill training centers, by offering health services, and by working with schools to offer additional tutorial services after school or on weekends, among many other things. Later, CBOs opened alternative schools. Over these 40-plus years, community-based organizations have learned a great amount about how to better serve low-income, ethnic/racial communities. For the most part, schools have ignored these agencies, which are rich in knowledge and experience. Schools should now become partners with CBOs and embrace them.

The fourth argument rests with a subset of elected public representatives. More persons who got their start as elected school board members are using this public service to help them get elected to other offices as city councilors, mayors, state representatives, and members of Congress. Also, persons who were once educators are running and winning public office. In addition, more persons of color are now elected representatives. To help the growing number of local, state, and national Latino public servants, the National Association of Latino Elected Officials (NALEO) was formed. The largest number of NALEO members is made up of Latino school board members. For certain, all Latino elected representatives say they want to improve the education of Latinos. But there are many other nonminority persons as well who are offering policy or legislation that works toward right-minded reform and change. Two quick examples come to mind. The DREAM Act proposes that children of undocumented residents be admitted into U.S. colleges and that their tuition be the same as that of U.S. citizens. Its premise is that children brought to the United States by their parents from Mexico should not be punished due to action they had no control over. The DREAM Act has yet to be passed in Congress.[8]

The second example offers hope that policy makers will start to get it right instead of considering and passing restrictive (wrong-headed) legislation. In 2004, Congressman Steny Hoyer from Maryland offered legislation[9] to fund full-service community schools. In stating his case for funding, he pointed out the pluses of full-service community schools: more and longer school days (more instructional time); seamless integration of academic, family, and health services to students and their families; the best use of resources; and strengthening of local communities (Tuttle, 2005).

Now that we know help is available and more persons can be recruited, let's offer up the three things being recommended for out-of-school learning: tutoring for academic skill building, mentoring for guided hands-on learning, and experienced-based learning. Many persons can do tutoring (e.g., college students, parents, high school students with middle school students, middle school students with elementary students). They can tutor reading, writing, speaking, and the basics in certain subject-matter topics, such as history. Equally, just as many persons can be mentors (e.g., business persons, professionals in various fields—medicine, law, engineering—and university or college students). The mentor introduces students to different experiences, gives explanations, and sketches out a lifestyle. Learning based on experience can range from accessing new places to work-study programs to formal internships. Each of these three experiential-based learning modes offers greater knowledge and skill depending on the amount of time spent in each.

Where can this out-of-school learning take place? All over, at city parks, recreation centers, zoos, and museums and in the work world. The impact that out-of-school learning can have on Latinos and other students who live in low-income communities can be tremendous. Rarely do these students visit international airports, harbors, corporate headquarters of banks, major law offices, courtrooms, or governmental offices. Exposure to such places and persons can be critical moments in the lives of young persons, opening up possibilities about what they can do as adults. These out-of-school learning events can be transforming experiences (i.e., student self-identity turns positive, and self-esteem grows into a healthy status). To gain an affective understanding of this point, I direct the reader to view the film *To Sir with Love* (1967).

To benefit from out-of-school learning, school personnel must absolutely engage others to help with the load and develop a way to track the advantages. The suggestions of tutoring and mentoring should force educators to think of education as all one system (i.e., prekindergarten, K–12, community colleges, four-year colleges, and graduate-level universities). All these different sections of the educational pipeline, artificially divided based on grade level (student's age), must not only communicate with each other but also cooperate on multiple elements, such as curriculum and student tracking, specifically academic achievement and family mobility. But in addition to making the education community's connections tighter, community-based organizations, municipal agencies, state departments, and teacher associations and unions must be drawn in. It is recognized that many of these listed institutions have their own bureaucracies and protocols. Thus, it will not be easy to work across these independent satellites in a more meaningful and helpful manner. But good effort will have to be made, and it must be started by the school leadership. Linkages at all levels between these two agencies (schools and other) will be necessary (e.g., board members, CEOs, school heads, teaching staff, support staff). At first, work will need to focus on frequent communications, not just at formal meeting times and through written communiqué but also by visiting each other at school and the workplace, to get to know what each associate faces on a daily and routine basis.

CONCLUSION

Schools consciously must increase the human characteristic of caring across the school campus. A 2005 study conducted by the University of Chicago recommends that schools ensure that every student feel close to at least one supportive adult in school (Voisin, 2005). One easy way to demonstrate caring is to capitalize on the Spanish language as a rich asset found in the community. In so doing, an equity of relationship between school and community will surface that will not only generate goodwill but more significantly will also add real support previously unseen and untapped. The two basic functions of schools, teaching and learning, will need to be expanded in thought and practice. Finally, reaching out to the many others wanting schools to improve will result in much-needed and wanted support and assistance.

NOTES

1. I became a charter board member of TEAC mainly because of its explicit inclusion of preparing "caring" teachers in its mission statement as well as its other perspective, that of critiquing teacher preparation programs as a whole and in a qualitative way, different from the NCATE way of measuring a set of input components as if the sum of the parts equaled the whole.

2. Interview conducted with Dr. Kino Flores, Tolleson Union High School District, Arizona, for manuscript published in *National Association of Secondary School Principals Bulletin*, 2001.

3. See article by Yvonne Wingett titled "2nd Generation Latinos Mean Wave of Change" in *Arizona Republic* newspaper, October 11, 2005.

4. I was first introduced to dual-language schools when visiting (1980s) Miami-Dade County schools and interviewing Dr. Rosie Castro Feinberg, director of a technical assistance center at the University of Miami. She later became an elected school board member and the only serving Latino on the board during her time.

5. For more understanding on this matter, I would recommend two sources: *Pygmalion in the Classroom* (Rosenthal & Jacobson, 1992) and *Perceiving, Behaving, and Becoming* (Combs, 1962).

6. For a quick peek into his approach, see "Mathematics Made Fun," a *Boston Globe* newspaper interview by reporter Lisa Palmer.

7. Two prominent persons quickly come to mind. One is film actor Anthony Quinn, whose parents came from Mexico and who attended Belvedere Junior High School in East L.A., and Antonia Hernandez, a graduate of the UCLA Law School and the former head of the Mexican American Legal Defense and Education Fund. (A side note: Quinn won an Academy Award for his supporting role in the film *Viva Zapata* and was nominated in the best actor category for playing *Zorba the Greek*.)

8. The DREAM Act, S. 1545, in the 108th Congress is a bipartisan legislation introduced by Senator Orrin Hatch (R-UT); in the House, the same bill is called the Student Adjustment Act (Cannon, R-UT-HR 1684). These two bills will be reintroduced into the 109th Congress for consideration and look favorable for passage.

9. Nebraska senator Ben Nelson cointroduced the Full-Service Community Schools Act of 2005. The FSCS Act authorizes $200 million for the fiscal year 2006 through 2010 for full-service community schools, which are public elementary and secondary schools that coordinate multiple federal, state, or local educational and social service programs with community-based organizations and public or private partnerships.

Part IV

EVALUATION, GOVERNANCE, AND LEADERSHIP

In many schools that have served Latino students of Mexican descent, too little assessment for school improvement has taken place. As such, bad decision making is in place; dysfunctional practices become embedded; and the vicious cycle of negative outcomes is strongly rooted. Consequently, schools cannot tinker around the edges to make repairs—they must be reinvented. Prevailing mind-sets that are negative toward students and families must be discarded. These destructive mental frameworks must be demolished and replaced with constructive thinking, thinking that mirrors creativity and imagination in educators. In turn, these new mind-sets can foster exploration and discovery in the minds of students. Chapter 7 outlines how formative evaluation can be used to reinvent schools by collecting useful information and by being a central part of strategic planning. Because schools are conservative institutions, tied to honoring the past, they are far too slow to seek out the new and the future. In an age of high technology, where the way we live is being radically reconfigured, it is imperative that schools incorporate the fast-evolving technological tools in their learning platform.

Chapter 8 expands the scope of rethinking how schools should be constituted and elevates the reinvention of schools to a higher level. Schools are organized far too much in the mold of a bureaucracy. Bureaucratic paperwork can lead people to rigid and counterproductive paths. Schools must replace this organizational structure to promote inclusion, openness, and flexibility. Comprehensively, we call for schools to be democratic in practice, not just in rhetoric, to liberate staff thinking and energies. Since the principles of democracy lie primarily in the hands and minds of school board members and the educational leadership, discussion is centered on these two groups. If schools are going to gain favor in the minds and hearts of students and parents, and if they are to gain support from community organizations and local businesses, they will have to create equitable relationships (i.e., replace the counterproductive relationship built on school superiority and family inferiority). To do so, schools will need to reach out to traditionally disenfranchised groups, provide them with representation, listen to their ideas and suggestions, and build trust by acting on their concerns. To gain additional and much-needed so-called private resources, schools will need to expand their services to serve more than just students. Expanding the mission of the school, reaching out to nonschool groups, and encouraging reinvention are under the province of governance and leadership.

Chapter Seven

Assessment for Human Development and Reinvention

For being known as places where learning occurs, the majority of schools (i.e., administrators, teachers, and support staff) do very little thinking about how to organize themselves so they can maximize their personnel strengths, utilize their time, and encourage cooperative efforts so that students learn. Typically, the process of evaluation is supposed to help fulfill this function. However, besides the fact that very little evaluation is being done, assessment is misdirected and has become counterproductive. Within the current era of accountability for the purpose of school reform, some would argue that data collection has become destructive. If schools for Latinos are to be reinvented for the better, evaluation will need to be redirected and become an integral part of school planning. To integrate assessment across the school, technology must be incorporated much more than in the past. This chapter discusses two areas: (1) evaluation for use in strategic planning and student learning and (2) technology as a tool in both school planning and student learning.

MOVING FROM LABELING TO HUMAN DEVELOPMENT ENVIRONMENTS

"Schools have to stop being insane! One interpretation of insanity is — schools continue to do the same thing over and over again, and then expect a much different outcome at the end of the year." This statement made by an experienced Latino superintendent[1] expresses both the frustration and understanding that many practitioners and scholars hold

103

about what has happened and is happening in schools serving Latino youths and their communities. I use this quote to emphasize that we must redirect how we think and do things when inventing new learning environments for Latino students, families, and communities. First, we can no longer continue to do the same things with evaluation. Summative evaluation must be deemphasized. This type of evaluation is done by schools only to satisfy the NCLB mandate. Supposedly, summative evaluation measures the amount of progress students have achieved, not necessarily how much they have learned. Standardized tests are administered toward the end of the academic calendar, and a score or percentile is provided after the school year has ended to compare results with other students. This type of evaluation provides very little useful information to schools, students, and parents about student learning. Instead it is used to label students as slow, average, or high achievers. With NCLB, these annual summative evaluation scores have also been used to label schools as failing, underperforming, or succeeding. The psychological damage this has done to students of color, who traditionally score low on such tests, has already been mentioned, but we would like to add that school labeling seems to be affecting school personnel in a very similar negative way.

More useful in purpose and practice is formative evaluation. Formative evaluation is used not to measure on a one-time basis (summative) but to collect information periodically to discern what is happening and why. The design of formative evaluation is different from summative. Formative evaluation is used to assess instructional programs, but it should and can be used to assess student learning, not just student achievement. In short, formative evaluation is a diagnostic tool, used to help understand what is working or not working, that will result in modifications or a whole new approach to the teaching and learning process. This type of evaluation is unlike summative evaluation, which is being used as a weapon directed at schools. While summative evaluation is being applied primarily to students (and results linked to teachers), formative evaluation can be applied to necessary elements that make for a healthy and successful school: (1) teachers, (2) administrators and instructional support staff, (3) resources, (4) environments, (5) curriculum, (6) expectations, (7) planning, and (8) nonacademic support.

SCHOOLS: EVALUATING TO ENHANCE THEMSELVES

Evaluation needs to occur at the whole-school level to promote strategic planning for the purpose of improving teaching and increasing learning. A few words about strategic planning before proceeding. Each year too many schools go through the school calendar in the customary fashion; the length of the school year is predetermined, holidays identified, staff development days designated, test days established, and so on. What little school-level planning that takes place can be considered superficial or hollow. Strategic planning provides many benefits. It forces staff to set goals and in so doing to reach consensus. Similarly it forces them to focus their time and energy on these goals in order to accomplish them. The process asks staff to identify the data to be collected throughout the school year to determine if their plan is the best way to reach their agreed-upon goals. Furthermore, it brings staff together on a regular basis throughout the semester to discuss information. Again, discussion on important matters forces the staff to confront reality, based on data that is not driven by emotions or impressions. This discussion generates feedback and an opportunity to reflect on actions. In short, this sequence of data collection and discussion is referred to as a feedback loop. If staff are satisfied with the progress, then the process can continue. If the data indicate they are not progressing sufficiently, then school personnel can alter what they are doing or make in-progress corrections and adjustments. Among the bigger benefits, strategic planning brings school staff together, allowing them to think of themselves as a collective, in partnership on agreed-upon purposes. They see themselves working cooperatively and interdependently. Thus they are succeeding as a community, not individually or as a subunit of the whole. They are focused and intent on helping each other. Last, they are thinking about what they are doing, not just doing the same thing over again through another school year. Instead, the strategic planning/evaluation process asks them to reflect on what they are doing. In the section that addresses technology, we will speak to the implementation of strategic planning/evaluation.

Returning to the matter of formative versus summative evaluation, I suggest more than just substituting formative evaluation for summative. I suggest that formative evaluation be activated in schools more creatively and usefully. That is, evaluation should not be seen as another noninstructional task, even if it is projected to be helpful. Remember, teachers are so overly occupied with accountability—and skeptical about evaluation because of the negative connotation—that formative evaluation should be presented in the most positive and rewarding way possible. In order to be consistent with previous themes proposed in this book, specifically to encourage school personnel to be more creative about their work so, in turn, they will be more imaginative in teaching Latino students to be critical thinkers, I will illustrate the utility of formative evaluation by identifying two areas: the arts in education and the use of time. Both are nontraditional in focus but have tremendous implications for human growth and development.

First, let's turn our attention to time. Without question we believe time is fixed, and therefore we can't manufacture more of it. After all, teachers often say, "If only I had more time with these kids [or on this topic], the results would be much better." This thought about having more time has truth to it because many policy makers and educators believe that much of our students' underachievement would be solved if we had a longer school year or a longer school day. Because the length of the school year is fixed to a certain number of days per year, and each school day is locked into so many hours per day, educators quickly pass up on evaluating the use of time. However, time is a precious resource that educators have under their control. There are at least two ways of evaluating the use of time in order to maximize this real resource. One is measuring how much time on task occurs during the school day. We all know there are distractions that take both the teacher and students away from instruction and learning. By doing simple data collection of time usage, schools can determine the time wasters and how much time is being lost. A quick remedy is to eliminate the structured activities that take time away from instruction to allow more time for teaching and learning.

While this will help, it will not help sufficiently. This type of study is equivalent to putting the finger in the dam. Instead, district leaders (board members and superintendents) and school building staff must boldly rethink the concept of time and learning. The prevailing understanding taught to teachers has been that time and learning have the following relationship: Learning is the variable, and time is the constant. That is, what we want the student to learn (commodity) varies (history, geography, math, science), and time is constant, or fixed. For simplicity, in secondary schools each of these subjects is given 55 minutes a day, since there are only six academic periods. But because the world has changed so much with regard to technology and information, time can now be considered as the variable and subject matter as the constant (Education Commission of the States, 2005). When educators interpret time in this different light, then their actions in utilizing time will be more creative and the managing of this resource will be more powerful, hopefully producing new arrangements, such as differentiated instruction, modular instructional units, and individual instruction. Specifically, by differentiating time for some subjects such as science, teachers can structure lessons that incorporate experimentation. Also, by utilizing the Internet and laptop computers, student learning time can be extended outside the school walls and the school day. More examples of how learning time can be rethought and used as well as how instruction can be more innovative is discussed when technology is addressed later in the chapter.

The second example that stresses the value and usefulness of evaluation and helps us rethink schools for Latinos is art in education. The arts in education have lost a great deal of importance with the emphasis on learning the fundamentals at the elementary school level and the emphasis by society on science and math at the secondary level. However, recent writings claim that the arts can facilitate deeper learning and more learning of traditional subjects and basic skills. One such authority who has promoted the use of evaluation via an art approach, connoisseurship, is convinced that art in teaching can produce greater learning among students in a variety of subjects (Eisner, 1985). First, through the arts, children can learn that problems have more than one solution, that a question may be answered in more than one way. Second, through the arts, teachers can demonstrate that complex forms of problem solving are seldom fixed. Third, arts make vivid the fact that neither words in their literal form nor numbers exhaust what children can come to know. Fourth, by working in the art medium, learners come to see and hear that small differences can have a large outcome. Fifth, by using the arts, students can express themselves in ways they cannot find in words. Sixth, via the arts, persons can have an experience that other sources do not permit (Eisner, 2002). With these as teasers to help teachers rethink how they can incorporate the arts in their teaching, different instruction should emerge in schools. Connect these elements together—formative evaluation, the use of arts in teaching, and the Mexican culture—and multiple ideas about learning should surface.

In closing this section on the greater utility of evaluation when reinventing schools for Latinos, one last recommendation is offered. Not only is school evaluation done meagerly, but when it is done it leaves out the very important group called students. This student exclusion occurs for many reasons (e.g., administrators believe students are too naive, teachers believe students will rely too much on their emotions), and it produces a climate that separates students from teachers and other school personnel. Students come to feel unwelcome and devalued. Omission adds to the prevailing tone of Latino schools, that of overly autocratic. To forge more inclusion and openness, it is recommended strongly that students participate in the evaluation studies. They have valuable insight to share, views typically different from teachers because of their status in schools. Oftentimes, students will reaffirm what some school staff already know is taking place. Allowing students to participate in school evaluation sends a message that what they think has merit, that they help shape what happens in schools, and that they are not solely the objects. Clearly, the more ways educators can get students to engage in school matters, the more buy-in students will have. The role of students beyond the classroom helps students see themselves as citizens in a community.

STUDENT LEARNING: EVALUATION FOR DEVELOPMENT

Narrowing our scope from school to student, and in keeping with the focus of evaluation for learning, not as measuring for achievement, two elements (both tied to each other) need to be stressed again. The first is that student evaluation must be centered to result in diagnosis. Student evaluation is a means of collecting information that informs teachers what and why students are capturing, not how much they are mastering. In other parts of the book I have discussed the consequences of testing for diagnostic purposes versus measurement purposes (e.g., minimize true/false, multiple choice, fill-in-the-blank types of tests). Instead, do more student observation and dialogue—oral questioning of the student. Second, by using evaluation to discover not measure, teachers have a solid basis for developing individualized programs of studies for students. Rather than restate the benefits of individualized instruction, space will be reserved to elaborate how this tailored instruction can take place. Suffice it to say that the well-worn statement of "one size does not fit all" needs to be internalized, and its counterpart needs to be put into practice — "start the learning where the child is," not where he or she is supposed to be in the graded curriculum.

INSERTING TECHNOLOGY TO RECONFIGURE LEARNING

While educational improvement has been marginal over the last two decades of school reform, one area that shows a dramatic advancement is technology. The Center for Educational Policy (2005) reports that in 1994 only 3% of the classrooms in public schools had access to the Internet. However, by the year 2003, the percentage had risen to a whopping 93%. As of this writing, it has probably increased even further, and more important, Internet access is becoming even easier. As recently as 10 years ago, outdated schools had to confront the high cost of wiring their buildings to permit for a modern infrastructure. In addition to this expense, there was the added cost of the computers that had to be purchased. Now, due to the rapid development in the technology arena, wireless is the main vehicle to access the Internet. On top of no cost for building reconfiguration, there may not even be a cost for access. At first, wireless meant setting up in "hot spots" such as coffee shops. Now whole cities (e.g., Tempe, Arizona) are working toward having a wireless umbrella.[2] When computers and Internet access are combined, both offer a powerful means of bringing learning to life and more meaningful ways of teaching and learning. In addition, instruction is no longer bound by the classroom and can extend beyond the school day. Also, this technology makes the management of instruction and school operations much easier and less time consuming. In fact, the new trends in technology can help tie together the various components proposed in this book. As technology advances, schools should partner with city governments and computer-related companies such as Dell and Microsoft.

Let's address how technology can lessen the burden of all the data collection and reporting mandated by NCLB. Then we will address how technology can free schools to be innovative and help reinvent themselves.

With the advent of school reform, for-profit ventures have sprung up. Among these varied private enterprises are those in school assessment. One such effort is SchoolNet, started in 1998 to help K–12 public school districts across the country make decisions based on data. In practice, the program enables school districts to integrate, access, and analyze student demographic and performance data at all levels, including the district, school, classroom, and individual student. These services help schools meet their yearly plans and goals and increase academic achievement. SchoolNet claims success with seven school districts across the country. The districts range in profile from Philadelphia to Corpus Christi, Texas. Philadelphia has more than 200,000 students in 276 schools with a $1.7 million budget. Corpus Christi has a large and growing ESL student population given its proximity to the U.S.-Mexico border. SchoolNet is identified herein not to promote it but simply to illustrate that schools can subcontract to meet the demands placed upon them by the federal No Child Left Behind Act. (To learn more about SchoolNet and its services, contact information is listed in chapter 9 in the section titled Program Assistance.) More important, NCLB has forced districts (particularly large urban and middle-class suburban school districts who have operating budgets) to create or enlarge an IT staff devoted to technology in order to collect school data and process school management procedures via computers and software programs.

While technology in schools has been used for data collection, creating reports, and managing school operations (e.g., tracking budget expenses, student attendance, scheduling, and employment status), its instructional uses are still underdeveloped and underutilized at all levels.[3] To stimulate greater use of technology in teaching and learning, it has been proposed that technology be used as a means of providing individualized instruction. Space limitation in this book does not permit us to detail how this can be done; however, what is known is that it can be done. The reader should look up the web page for SchoolNet to get one model. When individualization of instruction was being proposed in the late 1960s and early 1970s, the major problem was insufficient time and means to diagnose students, identify lessons, test for understanding, and keep track of all the necessary information for each student. However, with computers and software to test students, provide branching-type lessons, and keep a profile on each student, these major obstacles of the past are now gone.

Again with brevity, here are some more ideas of what can be done to promote a richer learning environment in schools. At the high school level, offer traditional courses online. One such effort is being undertaken at the Rapid City Academy, South Dakota. This alternative high school program has a high percentage of at-risk students due to transient lifestyles, teenage parenthood, high absentee rates, and low socioeconomic status. Online courses is one means by which the RC Academy provides quality education; others include individualized learning, flexible schedules, independent and group-led classes, and strategy-based learning. Of course there are problems as well as advantages. Some of the problems include limited access to computers and the Internet, limited face-to-face interaction, and loss of work due to system failure. However, among the advantages are flexibility and convenience (i.e., the freedom to chose when to work on class assignments) and the ability of students to think and reflect on content instead of having to respond instantly to a question asked in a classroom situation (Podoll & Randle, 2005).

At the middle school level, Modesto City Schools invested its Enhancing Education Through Technology grant funds to purchase Classroom Performance System (CPS), a wireless interactive response system, for four schools to use in math and science. Each CPS has a receiver, which is plugged into the teacher's classroom computer, and 40 response pads that students use during class to beam their responses via infrared signal. A projector is used to display each student response. From this information, teachers can complement questions with graphics and diagrams. In addition, the system can be programmed to automatically track grades and report student performances (Hines, 2005).

At the elementary level, Hoover Elementary, in Calumet City, a suburb of Chicago, turned to technology to solve the problem of teaching students of widely varying ability and with a 64% mobility rate who are placed in the same classroom. The school purchased LeapFrog School-House so students could have personalized coaches, teachers have more time to work one on one, and students are able to engage and follow their individual learning plans. How? Books become interactive when used with LeapPad and QuantumPad personal learning tools (PLTs). The system includes an electronic stylus and headphones. If a student cannot pronounce the word or does not know its meaning, he or she taps the word with the stylus and a personal audio coach sounds out the word and provides a definition. Pictures in the book become interactive as well. For the slower reader, reading is no longer embarrassing or tedious. With the earphones, only the child knows what words he or she does not know. Also, slow readers can read less demanding (commonly called lower grade-level) books without the stigma of being underachieving. Finally, LeapFrog is seen by teachers as a great way to teach English language learners because it provides individualized instruction and allows for more one-on-one time (Mollin, 2005).

Using video games and using computers to connect with Latino parents are the last two ideas presented herein to motivate school staff to reinvent themselves. Ever wonder why it is that children and even teenagers will spend hour after hour playing video games, yet they can't sit still for 15 or 30 minutes to do their homework? It is not because the games are easy but because they are challenging and engaging. These games need to be challenging in order to capture the interest of the kids. They force the game player to problem solve to win or succeed in mastering the game. By being good at the game, children find enjoyment (Gee, 2003). So designers of video games need to develop interactive learning games that are both interesting to the eyes and ears and provide challenging options with varying degrees of difficulty for young learners. The game player will have the opportunity to explore and discover concepts by playing the game again and again. Teachers should take advantage of video games in the classroom for learning purposes. (Remember the math teachers who resisted the use of pocket calculators in the classroom.) With video games, teachers may one day face the situation of having to urge students to stop their learning assignments!

While the digital divide between the haves and have nots still exists (i.e., low-income families are less likely to have a computer in their homes) (Fairlie, 2005), this situation may be another opportunity to exploit when it comes to getting closer with parents and families. New Latino schools under the banner of being full service and community based should prioritize to purchase laptop computers and set up a computer resource room. At the same time they should team up with local city-operated public libraries to provide computer access to families. Also, securing computers for parental use should be a high priority for the school to seek partnership with a business firm. Once schools have computers and Internet access, they can teach parents how to use them and more important how to access the Internet. Think of all the possibilities the Internet offers for parents to learn English and for English-speaking students to learn Spanish; for schools to be in touch with parents and vice versa; for attracting persons into schools; for school staff to learn more about families when they are on campus; and for teachers and parents to use the computers as equals.

CHANGE: AS A NATURAL WAY OF REINVENTING

This chapter began by mentioning that the accountability movement is counterproductive—if not detrimental—for Latino students and schools. It can also be stated that school reform has not promoted constructive change for schools, and particularly for Latino schools. While many publicly elected representatives believe that accountability leads to school reform, it is not surprising to many educators that this is a misguided belief (Sarason, 1990). Therefore, we have shown how evaluation, data collection, and technology can be means to produce change that will reinvent Latino schools for the better. In closing this chapter, some additional information about change is offered to help in the metamorphosis of schools.

For dramatic purposes, think of demolishing the mental scaffolding school staff have built in their minds. This purging is what Harvard economist Joseph Schumpeter called creative destruction[4] (Doyle, 2005). Now replace the mind-set with new positive models where every Latino student and family have assets, all have and bring a desire to learn, and it is just up to teachers to find the right methods. How do we get persons to shed ingrained ideas, especially when they can't admit they possess them? And after getting persons to reject these destructive views, how do we get them to embrace the concept of change and to insert these new constructive beliefs? The reinvention process can begin either directly or indirectly.

Indirectly, the school leadership must ask the instructional staff a series of questions. Are we teaching to a level where students are achieving? Can we say that achievement gains represent real learning? Are we happy in our work? Are we meeting students' and families' needs? Are we respected for our efforts by students, parents, and community members?

Does our community see us as helpers? Do businesses and others want to be associated with us? Are we seen in a favorable light, as successful?

Given the current state of most schools, the answers may reveal an unsatisfactory set of conditions. If so, the leadership can start a series of discussions with staff to urge them to go in a new direction, present a new vision, and commit to working to reinvent the school.

Directly, the leadership states the obvious: All the major indicators tell schools that they are not getting students to achieve, let alone learn and be critical thinkers. Schools are seen as unsuccessful and educators as contributing to the problem. We can no longer try to explain away the situation because of the lack of resources, unsupportive families, or poor neighborhoods. The public only sees these explanations as denial and blaming everyone else. Therefore, all school district educators must take the pledge. A new manifesto must be posted, accepted, and worked on. What makes up the manifesto?

1. Each school must become a community of believers! We believe every child comes to school with assets. All parents want their children to succeed. Teachers can teach any student to learn. Where there is a will, there is a way.
2. Schools can control their destiny. They are not victims. They can control time and get more resources. There is no limit to their ingenuity.
3. Schools can enrich their human capital in many ways, but primarily by well-conceived, meaningful, and continual staff development programs. The staff is the energy and powerhouse.
4. Schools can empower themselves by discarding their bureaucratic structure and assuming characteristics of a learning organization. Creativity, exploration, and flexibility are necessary and encouraged.
5. Schools must model inclusion by outreach and establish relationships based on equity that will promote partnerships.
6. Schools must put students first—no child is expendable! As such, learning must be student centered in classrooms. Schools are organized to serve students, not administrators. Administrators cannot put loyalty to the organization before students; teachers cannot put their self-interest (teacher unions) before students (Read "Which Side Are You On?" Peterson, 1995); and school board members cannot put their reelection before students.

7. Leaders must act as entrepreneurs, linking their schools with others in ways that result in support. A stronger connection must be with community. The driving source for this networking is schools must have a bigger mission—they must become full-service institutions.

8. Educators who serve communities of color must believe that education is a social process, much broader than providing formal instruction. As such, educators must learn about the Mexican culture and infuse it throughout the entire school. Embracing language (the use of Spanish by all) and the arts will help greatly in creating a welcoming environment.

9. Hold the highest of expectations for students, for yourself, and for schools. *Sí se puede*. No matter the odds, they can be overcome. Excellence is reachable. The key to reaching excellence is the road traveled. Stay committed to the expectation.

10. Technology provides the tools of today and will help in creating engaged learning as well as with strategic planning and data-driven decisions. Don't shy away from technology—seek it out. Ask how it can help teachers teach and students learn. How can it help provide a richer learning environment?

The previous 10 elements are interrelated and should be taken as a whole. They should be used as guides or in outline form. Each school or district should articulate each one to tailor the manifesto to fit their particular situation. To help schools get assistance from other practitioners, see the resources listed in chapter 9.

CONCLUSION

Reinvention, not reform, is necessary if schools are truly to promote human development of Latino students. Formative evaluation for diagnostic purposes used throughout the entire school and school year is one means of reinvention. The value of ongoing data collection and analysis requires that all staff come together to dissect progress or lack thereof, not to reinforce stereotypic perceptions. In these frequent meetings, assessment of reaching previously agreed-upon goals forges a sense of community. Also, school evaluation demands that students be included in some part of the progress. In addition, technology can facilitate school reinvention by efficiently managing all the data collection but, more importantly, can make it possible to individualize instruction for students, extend the amount of time students can spend on learning, and become a means to bring parents and teachers together. Lastly, reinvention permits schools to pledge allegiance to a manifesto that redirects their thinking and practice in a creative way.

NOTES

1. Waldemar "Bill" Rojas, former superintendent in New York City, San Francisco, and Dallas, shared this observation at a meeting convened by HBLI in Phoenix, Arizona, November 2004. All in attendance were in full agreement.

2. The cell phone provider Verizon is advertising on television that they have entire cities covered via broadband connection and not just hot spots within the city.

3. For a quick read on the development and use of information technology in schools, see "The Evolution of Student Information Systems," by Robert Darby and Tim Hughes, 2005, *T.H.E. Journal, 33*(3), 38.

4. Creative destruction was defined as replacing old and inefficient processes or products with new, novel, and efficient processes or products. Without creative destruction, the many wireless technology products such as cell phones and the Internet would never have been created.

Chapter Eight

Hbding True tdDemratic Principles

This chapter is about upholding and staying true to the principle that this country was founded upon: democracy. Flowing from this democratic principle is governance. Closely associated with governance is leadership. Therefore the contents of this chapter are targeted at school board members as the formal governors; school leaders (superintendents, principals, teacher association heads); civic, community, and business leaders; and state and nationally elected officials, who represent the interests of and who work to respond to the needs of neighborhoods and local communities. Consequently, discussion will center upon the following themes: (1) openness through the development of trust and equitable relationship building, (2) inclusion through partnership and participation of parents and others, (3) representation by balancing majority and minority interests, (4) qualities of leaders for Latino schools and school districts, and (5) the leaders' roles in buttressing the change process when they act to create new schools. Fundamentally, this chapter calls for schools to show basic fairness and promote parental and community involvement, especially in decisions that affect the lives of the students.

AN EDUCATED CITIÆNRY WL SUSTAIN DEMOCRACY

Thomas Jefferson, a key architect of the U.S. Constitution, believed firmly that if the experiment in democracy was to survive, the United States had to have an educated population. The newly formed United States would be governed not by aristocrats but by the people. People would rule by practicing the democratic ideals of (1) everyone is equal, or "one man, one vote"; (2) governance through representation, or "no taxation without representation"; (3) the majority rules; (4) the rights of the minority shall be protected, or the rule of law; and (5) freedom of expression, or every person can be heard. To educate the populace so democracy could flower, each state in the union was charged with the responsibility of establishing schools that were free or publicly supported. These schools were to be governed by town leaders. As the union grew in number of states and with the passage of time, public schooling in north America came to mean (1) free education for all students, (2) public accountability at the local level through formal elections, (3) equal educational opportunity for all students, and (4) the teaching and practice of democratic principles.

Today, the school district remains as one of the purest democratic institutions in the United States. The majority of schools is governed by elected citizens who reside in the district's boundaries. Among their many powers, they have authority to make policy and hire all school staff. As elected officials, they are representatives, obligated to listen to the views of parents who have children enrolled in and attending schools in the district, to consider matters, and make decisions. Since they do not need to leave their residences to conduct their responsibilities and fulfill their obligations (like state legislators traveling to the state capitol or congressional representatives moving to Washington, DC), they can be held accountable rather easily and reached immediately. Much of their business must be conducted in open sessions, with the business agenda posted in advance and a formal process that allows for public input and participation. While school boards in wealthy and middle-class communities uphold representative democracy, in low-income and in ethnic/racial communities of color, constituent representation and the principles (if not the spirit) of democracy have been minimal. Because democracy has been marginalized for communities of color, it is fair to say (and studies have revealed) that these schools have been weakened considerably. Parent input has been ignored, student learning depressed, and community resources undeveloped; worst of all, generations of students have had their futures wasted.

If we are going to make schools effective places where Latino students learn to their full potential and communities are served to make the quality of life for families enriching, then school districts will have to uphold the democratic ideals and principles in Latino communities. It is now long past due to place schools in the minds and hands of the people who care deeply for their children (called parents) and of community leaders who care greatly about their neighborhoods and communities. Regrettably, I cannot say that we can *return* schools into the hands of Latino elected representatives since history reports that our numbers have been minuscule, and even now the number of Latino school board members is still very small (only 3.8%), demonstrating underrepresentation when compared with student enrollments (see Figure 8.1). Given the number of obstacles in place that prevent more Latinos from getting elected to serve as school board members (such as at-large elections, especially in large urban school districts), it is important that school boards and superintendents find ways of ensuring greater Latino representation.[1] In the next section of this chapter, more will be said about how we can promote and get more Latino representation. Representation is necessary for a number of reasons. One, it establishes the feeling and reality of inclusion. Two, it permits more people to become stakeholders. Three, it generates more willingness to work together. Four, it opens up more access to resources, both human and material. In short, the entire community joins in and believes they are in a partnership. The more involved persons are in educational matters (across the spectrum), the more informed they will be and the more they will come to similar conclusions and develop creative solutions.

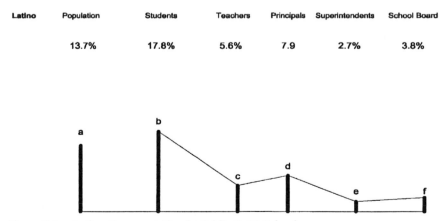

Latino	Population	Students	Teachers	Principals	Superintendents	School Board
	13.7%	17.8%	5.6%	7.9	2.7%	3.8%

Figure 8.1. Latino Representation in Public K–12 Schools

Sources: American Association of School Administrators, personal communication (November 2005); Hess (2002); National Center for Educational Statistics (2003); National Commission of Educational Statistics (2005); U.S. Census Bureau (2005).

The biggest advantage of practicing democracy within ethnic and racial minority communities is that it forges a different formal relationship between school people and community members, one built on fairness and equality. Historically, the relationship between schools and ethnic/racial minority communities has been one of inequality based on the laden status of superior versus inferior or expert educator versus laymen parent. This attitude, as subconscious as it may be, has led to many unwanted consequences. One negative result was the missionary view. Educators who served in low-income, Spanish-speaking Latino communities developed a view that they knew what was best for these kids. That is, given the many societal limitations these students would have to face, administrators and teachers depressed their expectations and in so doing limited many a student's future. As a result, minority schools became more of a sorting institution than a place of learning (Spring, 1976).

GOVERNANCE

In a presentation to the Massachusetts Legislature in 1961, just 11 days before taking the oath of office as the 35th president of the United States, John F. Kennedy said the following:

> Today the eyes of all the people are truly upon us and our government, in every branch, at every level—national, state and local—[government] must be a city upon a hill constructed and inhabited by men aware of their grave trust and their great responsibilities.

If we substitute the word *education* for the word *government*, this quote holds true today 45 years later. Because of this perception, President Kennedy injected a country with vigor and launched the United States into new frontiers. He did so because without question society was changing. While his presidency will be remembered for many accomplishments, it will be heralded for its spirit of Camelot. Kennedy brought the best and brightest minds into government service, tackled difficult problems, and assured the public that the future was still very much in front of us and that we were in control of our own destiny. In short, he believed in inclusion by making people become stakeholders; he believed that problems could and would be solved. Persons in service of their country would improve the world.

With this parallel situation, school boards and the district leadership will need to work on creating a similar Camelot mind-set for their schools. In this section we concentrate on the role of the school board. Since school boards are the embodiment of democracy through their status of governance, it is incumbent upon them (although not solely) to set the tone for creating welcoming, full-service, community-based schools. Two major ways of bringing about a new districtwide attitude of *sí se puede* are dos and don'ts for school boards. First the do list, since it is longer.

First, develop and maintain the feeling of trust at all levels and among all groups. This relationship must be cultivated particularly between two groups—teacher associations and community-based organizations that represent parents—because of their long-standing at-odds status. But establish a better trust level with other groups as well in light of the historical benign neglect of support staff at the school level (custodial and cafeteria) and others such as teacher aids. Keep in mind that you will have to overcome many years of mistrust. Trust building is not instantaneous; it must be earned and will require time. How can school boards start to turn around the mistrust? Say clearly what you will do, and do what you say. Keep your promises. Be consistent in saying what you will do, and continue to do what you say. Trust will naturally lead to forging relationships, the second element on the list. How can you bond better with district parents and community leaders? Through frequent contact, sharing information with each other, and expressing what you believe in and the goals you have. By listening to community leaders and parents express their desires. By adopting goals that include the parents' and community's expectations and wishes. Relationships based on trust, frequent contact, two-way communication, and finding agreement on common goals can lead to partnerships, the third element. Partnerships will facilitate working together on common goals and problems. Collaboration and cooperation will form equal partnerships, based on each partner bringing and having different strengths.

These elements of trust, relationships, and partnerships are nice in concept, but how does one foster them in a large urban school district? The fourth thing to do is establish ways of reorganizing the district and managing the schools, specifically by decentralizing the school district and starting site-based councils. As is well known, school boards are small in member numbers (five, seven, and nine members). Urban school districts are large in size (number of schools, number of students enrolled, number of staff, and so on) and very diverse (due to geography and wealth status). These differences mean that representation is lost for some communities (typically low income), and the interests of others (wealthy) are overrepresented. For these and other reasons, large urban school districts have been forced to try ways of making their school districts smaller. However, while the move toward decentralization has been sparked by complaints of inadequate representation, school districts have used decentralization more for better management than for representation. Because of this somewhat distorted purpose, decentralization has not worked well. Similarly, site-based councils were promoted to form partnerships by having parents and community leaders become part of the school management team, which included teachers and was headed by the school principal. However, these site-based councils did not flourish substantially because people did not understand their new roles and schools did not provide sufficient time to allow these school-based management teams to get established and evolve naturally. Nonetheless, it has been proposed throughout the book that by including others and getting more people involved, the enterprise becomes stronger and richer. The more human capital a district can get to become stakeholders, the better off the district and in turn the students and families will be.

Fifth, school board members should promote accountability but with a new emphasis. A recent survey (Arens, 2005) conducted to uncover what parents and other community members, particularly those in underrepresented populations, think about educational accountability found that those surveyed believe that parents, community members, and students should also be held accountable (in addition to schools) for student success. Hence, school boards already have a head start to build from (i.e., the responsibility of developing good and healthy schools so that students learn more than in the past goes well beyond the school district). However, in this same survey, Spanish-speaking community members expressed disbelief in teachers when they use the phrase "all children can learn." This is a reminder that both students and parents can still gauge the level of truth expressed by school personnel and that school personnel still harbor unwarranted stereotypes, and these beliefs go unexpressed by teachers. Sixth, in setting the proper tone for rebuilding, school boards must be the instigators for change. They can no longer be in a reactive mode, responding to crisis, formed out of the many years of perpetuating the status quo. As school boards, they are well positioned to recognize local conditions and identify impediments. As such, they must be in the forefront of the necessary change; they must be the shapers of change, change that will meet their demanding needs. They will need to become change agents themselves in order to instill the mind-set for change to redefine schools within their leadership, starting with the superintendent. Just as change was mentioned before (e.g., in chapter 7), more will be said about change later in this chapter.

Now for the list of don'ts. School boards must not be micromanagers. Don't involve yourself in the daily operation of schools. Leave the running of the schools to the hired professionals. If complaints come in to you, pass them on to your superintendent and ask him or her to follow up (but don't tell the superintendent *how* to follow up). Your role is to formulate policy, a framework under which the district is to apply its capital, human, and material resources; to set the goals and priorities of the district; and then to monitor through your superintendent the district's progress. Second, school board members should not become insulated from their constituents, parents, and community leaders. They should not become overly reliant on information coming solely from the superintendent. Nor should they place more weight on information coming from the superintendent or the school staff without having discussion about the information presented. Third, when monitoring progress, school boards should not simply have reports given to them at the start and end of the year. Instead, they should receive quarterly reports and engage in discussion as to why the outcomes are as they are. Why are they good for one school and not another? What can and needs to be done to improve certain schools? Again, board discussion is for the purpose of learning where the district is with regard to the goals set and what contributions the board can make. Finally, school boards should not act as individuals. Instead they must act as one. The board has vested authority; individual board members do not have the authority to act independently of the board.

POLICIES THAT WLL SET A NEWIRECTION

Policies are important, and they should be adopted to meet the prevailing conditions facing the local school district. Because school districts vary from each other, it would be inappropriate to list policies that should be adopted for all districts with Latino students, especially of Mexican descent. However, one example of a new policy for school boards to seriously consider adopting is being offered because of the instructional and learning consequences for Latino students.

The national profile of Latino students in two types of educational programs is skewed and unfavorable. Specifically, Latino students are considerably overrepresented in special education programs, classified as learning disabled, and equally underrepresented in talented and gifted programs. School boards should establish a simple policy that states their student body should be distributed in the bell curve (i.e., the majority of the student body should be in the middle quadrants, with equal numbers at the low end and the high end of the curve). After adopting this commonsense policy, school boards should ask district leadership to develop definitions and criteria that would place students proportionately in each of the four quadrants. Too many Spanish-speaking students, because they do not know the English language sufficiently, are being labeled as learning disabled. This special education term is defined as any student who has difficulty using language in speaking, listening, reading, spelling, and writing, among other things (PL 94-142, 1975). Supposedly, these difficulties are due to a physiological disorder and not due to a language difference. Yet many Latino students are misplaced in this category because of their language usage. It may be easier to eliminate the misplaced students in special education than to place more Latino students in the gifted and talented program at the other end of the quadrant.

The opposite end of the bell-shaped curve is for high achievers, college prep programs, and advanced placement courses, as well as for gifted students in other areas besides academics. If school staff begin to discuss and widen their interpretation of the placement requirements for the high-end quadrant, more students will be identified. Clearly, common sense tells us that within any population there is a normal distribution of talent all along the bell curve. Coupled with the attitude that there are many more students who can achieve if motivated, challenged appropriately, and given additional assistance, then we should see more Latino students at the higher end.

I end this section with a reminder that democracy is messy. There are so many variables involved with school boards, and these variables determine the quality of their governance. Years of service, understanding the role of the school board, different personalities, different interests, constituent support—each of these factors can and to some degree do determine the quality of togetherness and effectiveness of school boards. Because of these variables, it is important to select a school board president who is senior and experienced, and the board must select a superintendent who can provide leadership and management. Both of these positions, school board president and school district superintendent, are the glue and standard that will establish the level of success in creating vibrant places of learning.

DYNAMIC LEADERSHIP FOR NEW SCHOOLS

In a democratic country, governmental leaders and persons heading societal institutions that serve the public good play a vital role in bringing to life these noble principles. So attention will now turn to school leadership, primarily district superintendents and school building principals. When speaking to leaders of schools that are in low-income communities of color, it becomes apparent that their job is more difficult and requires a different set of qualities than in middle-income, suburban schools. There are other ways to differentiate the leadership qualities required of these leaders. I propose 10 qualities that will serve schools well where the majority of the students are Latino of Mexican descent:

1. Empathic = compassionate
2. Creative thinker = out-of-the-box thinking
3. Ethical = social justice
4. Driven = passionate
5. Optimistic = against all odds, we will win
6. Entrepreneur = developer of venture capital
7. Energetic = explorer

8. Value added = inventor
9. People person = *con un abrazo de amistad*
10. Change agent = social architect

These 10 qualities are not in order of priority, but each is vital to have. By describing each characteristic, its value should become obvious. Readers familiar with leadership qualities such as those found in the literature (Covey, 1989) will find both overlap and differences.

Empathy, not sympathy, will motivate superintendents and principals to take action that reconstructs schools to be more effective. Persons who can genuinely relate to the many negative experiences or consequences that Latino youths experience on a daily basis are much more apt to eliminate the conditions that have brought about this banal situation. Latinos who have been through the public school experience as students and later return as teachers and become successful in moving up the educational ladder are more likely to care deeply for the present generation of students. Experiencing firsthand what Latino youths undergo as students is no assurance that they know what should and needs to be done to undo the wrong. But they are more likely to reach this higher plane of feeling (i.e., compassion). Because of this background, Latino professionals should be given serious consideration when they are in the pool of candidates for decision-making positions.

Institutionalized, deeply rooted practices that produce poor students are unlikely to be corrected by traditional institutional thinking. Instead, fresh ideas and out-of-the-box thinking are desperately in demand. Persons who interpret actions differently from the mainstream are more likely to come up with solutions different from the conventional viewpoint. One good example to support this last point is the newspaper surveys about police and minority communities. Surveys show that persons of color view the actions of the police differently from what police express as their justification and what whites conclude. The historical ways Latinos have been impacted by schools has facilitated their differing viewpoints. While there is more propensity for educational leaders of color to think differently, what is needed are creative thinkers.

With so much emphasis on academic results, the ethical dimension of leadership has fallen off the horizon. There is always a reminder in the professional literature that calls for ethical leadership to return (Shapiro &

Stefkovich, 2005). Only recently, there appears to be a call for a revival of ethics (see Bolman & Deal, 2001). School boards under tremendous pressure to reform schools and get better outcomes want superintendents who are solid managers and who can control the many levels of a complex organization. In turn, superintendents are selecting principals who can supervise staff, account for expenses, meet deadlines, and produce reports. However what is badly needed in schools where minority students make up the majority of the student body are leaders who insert an ethical dimension in their decisions and actions. By this I mean most if not all persons in educational leadership roles have ethics, but they are not incorporating them into their daily responsibilities, especially in these Latino schools. For example, ethical leaders would not allow for a disproportional number of minority students each year to be reported for breaking school rules, to receive punishment such as suspension or expulsion without trying to change the situation. Ethical leaders would find it wrong for minority students to continually be scored as low achievers. Ethical leaders would find it unjust for their children to be shortchanged because the state does not fully fund its state formula. Leaders with ethical standards would find it unconscionable to have students drop out of school before graduation. In short, leaders who practice their ethics would be driven to act to rectify these wrongful circumstances.

Latino schools need leaders who are mentally driven. Leaders who will not accept the status quo, not let things stand as they are. Even if the circumstances are good, they are not satisfied. They have a will to make things better and to strive for excellence. To be the best they can be and to motivate others to do the same. They will not take no for an answer when getting what they believe is needed. They mirror overachievers. They are driven in a way that New Leaders for New Schools (2005) states as "a relentless drive to lead an excellent urban school, and an unyielding belief in the potential of every child to achieve academically at high levels." In short, their thirst is never quenched.

"Can do" is another credo that these leaders live by. They are optimistic. They not only view the glass as half full but also want to fill it to the top. However, they are realists, not "pie in the sky" optimists. They don't ignore the hardships and difficulties; in fact, they factor them in, but they don't allow barriers to defeat their spirit. These leaders believe in themselves and in others. With creative thinking, a sound plan of action, and the drive over an extended period of time, they will succeed in reaching their goals. Their optimism translates to others to become a community of believers!

Any person in a leadership role, particularly in schools where populations of color are the majority, must be an entrepreneur. In the late 1960s and the 1970s, African Americans were being selected as superintendents of large urban school districts across the country. In analyzing why this was happening, one conclusion was that school boards were desperate (the crisis was too great), and more important, the district was bankrupt. The problems were so overwhelming and the district's operating budget so anemic that the school boards and communities needed individuals who could do more with less. The financial resource picture is still the same. Some argue that financial conditions are worse now than before; others state that the situation is better than in the past; but all agree that economically, school districts with students of color are still underfunded. Even after successful court rulings that declared state funding formulas as inequitable, some state legislatures respond slowly and do not comply faithfully. School districts with "minority" student populations as the majority are still insufficiently funded. Therefore, these schools and districts will need to appoint leaders who can identify and secure nontraditional resources in order to provide adequate instructional services. They will need to learn how to find investors willing to provide capital to enhance the schools.

Because it takes so much more effort to create anew than to maintain what exists, leaders will need to have ample energy. Leaders must be healthier than in previous generations, and they should attend to both their physical and mental fitness. The workdays are longer, and they extend beyond the workweek. School superintendents of large, urban low-wealth districts and building principals of overcrowded, underfunded schools are now on call 24/7. Even the days off during school holidays and short administrative summer vacations no longer are taken by these school leaders. With such a demand on their time and efforts, these persons must be energetic to the nth degree. Leaders under these high demands will have to learn to relieve stress and to replenish their spirits. Physical exercise on a routine basis and some kind of outside relaxation is highly recommended.

Leaders of community-based schools must add value to the enterprise. They must contribute in order to get something in return. Leaders of

Latino schools cannot be satisfied with just fulfilling their tasks satisfactorily (e.g., keeping schools open and running without incident, providing safe environments), even under the most trying conditions. The times and conditions clearly and loudly call for new and better schools. Leadership must provide a new vision, set goals, find more resources, empower staff, encourage students, help develop communities, and more. In short, leaders strengthen, improve, and build up. Or returning to the glass is half full analogy, they not only add more water to the glass so more can drink, they also find ways to enrich the water with healthy minerals so that those who drink are better for it.

It cannot be forgotten that education is a human enterprise. Fundamentally, it is one person helping another person to grow. Typically, the assistance is face to face or person to person. It has been stated earlier in the book that the Mexican American culture values human interaction highly. Most cultures judge a person by the way he or she engages on a one-to-one basis or in a group. More and more school leaders must demonstrate good public speaking skills, but listening is equally important. School leaders will need to feel comfortable with Latinos and at the same time make Latinos feel at ease when talking to such authority figures. By having an embracing personality, school leaders will be better able to enlist the assistance needed to get the big job done.

Above all, leaders of Latino schools must think of themselves as agents for change. Change in any organization at any time, even under good circumstances, is the most demanding task of all. When former president Bill Clinton was asked in 2005 how he thought Wal-Mart (headquartered in Arkansas) would overcome its current public problems and continue to be even more successful in the future, his reply was surprising: "They will keep on doing what made them mighty. This will bring them down! They won't think of ways to improve [change]." Change is resisted at any time, when things are going well and even when things are going badly. The only time change is favored by people is when someone else has to undergo it. So what must school superintendents and principals do to bring about a redefinition of Latino schools? First, read about the process and dynamics of change. The literature, particularly of corporate America in the 1980s, has a wealth of information (see the book *In Search of Excellence* by Peters & Waterman, 1982). Second, keep in the forefront of your mind what Kantor (2005) states: "Discover the things your people really care about, and see how the change can connect with their goals. . . . Conduct lots of conversations about hopes and aspirations."

ORGANIZATIONAL QALITIES

Just as it has been recommended that leaders must have certain qualities for new Latino schools to be invented, schools must also have certain frameworks in place to be successful in their progression to becoming student-centered, community-based, full-service facilities. These five organizational attributes are drawn from the book *Schools that Learn* (Senge, 2005).

First, all persons in an organization (adults and youths) have mental models that dictate how they see the world. We have already spoken at length in chapters 2 and 3 of the mental model that the professionals within Latino schools must possess. As a reminder, teachers, counselors, principals, district office support staff, superintendents, and school board members must believe that families want their children to succeed and are willing to help; that communities are vibrant and filled with resources, both human and financial; that students bring with them assets and are not deficient; that the Mexican culture positively influences student learning and thus must be integrated into the school; and that schools must turn away from the industrial model and the dysfunctional purpose of Americanizing Latino students. Instead, the mental model to be adopted is that education takes place in a cultural and social context, and others besides teachers can and do play a significant role in teaching children and youths. In short, it takes a whole village to educate individuals, and due to the constant and increasing societal changes that keep occurring, plurality, diversity, and flexibility must be the constants of the school process.

Second, interaction and relationships revolve around these subconscious mental models. The old ways that school teachers used to interact with parents and that administrators used to interact with community persons are minimally useful. It was one way—in English and typically in telling mode, usually focusing on what's wrong. Similarly, when administrators and school board members related to community leaders and community-based organizations, it was on a paternal basis. These approaches produced negative interactions and inequitable relationships, which in turn were counterproductive, causing friction between schools and those they were established to serve. In many schools across the country, where the interaction is two-way—both Spanish and English, and listening and sharing—the engagement is more informative and pleasant for both groups. Also where the relationship is based on a partnership, both school and community persons feel equal, with an attitude that both have strengths and contributions to make. In short, they are all stakeholders, and all can help each other.

Third, there must be thorough communication, both vertical and horizontal. Throughout the book we have stressed the need for the inclusion of Spanish in schools, not just in the classroom with students but also in interacting with support staff, in speaking with parents, and in communicating with persons in the community. By using as much Spanish as possible throughout the school, each and every day, loud messages are sent. One, educators are demonstrating that they are making an effort to communicate with parents and students by learning their native language. Two, it signals that the Spanish language is just as good as English. Three, by school personnel making the effort to learn Spanish, they become more knowledgeable about their students, their parents, and their families and more appreciative of the Mexican culture. By speaking Spanish, school personnel will no longer be hesitant to speak with parents, and vice versa. Furthermore, if schools provide English instruction for parents, parents will be more receptive to speaking with administrators and school board members. So there will be more vertical communication taking place, not just at the school building level but at the district level as well. As both sides become more comfortable in talking with each other, they will get to know one another better on a personal level, promoting more and more contact with each other. This will result in deeper and fuller communication.

Fourth, learning takes place in context, and teaching must be connected. I have proposed that learning takes place beyond the confines of the four classroom walls. Typically, formal education has been constricted so that it happens only at school in a classroom. This definition is more suitable to what we call schooling. However, education is much broader than this interpretation. Youths learn from parents, their extended family members, their neighborhoods, the mass media, and so on. Therefore, I have proposed that the learning of Latino students of Mexican descent takes place in a Mexican American cultural context, and as such the teaching must be connected to this social cultural context. Instead of continuing with past practices (e.g., rejecting the Mexican culture by punishing the use of Spanish by students), schools should incorporate the Mexican culture along with the American culture as much as possible. Teachers and administrators should extend themselves beyond the school grounds and buildings to involve community and business people as partners in the formal educational process.

Fifth, learning is driven by vision (the big picture) and relevance (purpose in a person's life). America's future is very different from what it used to be. During the industrial age, America needed workers to manufacture products and cheap labor to harvest its agricultural crops. Also, it had a much more stratified economic society. America's future is now based on high technology, the global economy, and information. It now needs a highly educated workforce, one that is flexible, able to adapt and adopt new ways, and able to retool itself for a rapidly changing economy. Schools can no longer afford to fail their large population of color. The business world will not allow it. Already we see corporate leaders issuing reports of what schools and colleges need to do to prepare the future workforce of this nation. We have proposed that schools reach out to the communities they serve and to the business sector for partnerships that will put students into business settings. Students placed in internships will be mentored and will learn by doing. Through this process, students can find individual purpose and seek relevance in their learning.

CONCLUSION: REDEFINITION AND LIBERATION, NOT REFORM

Earlier in the chapter when discussing leadership qualities, being a change agent was identified. We return to this topic because of its importance to the book's focus of creating communities of believers. First, it must be restated that reform is not the purpose of this book, not just because reform has been interpreted to mean setting higher standards and testing for accountability but also because reform is too shallow and too negative. What I and others are calling for is grander and more noble—and better suited for today's educator. Educators are being challenged by America's changing status to invent a new way of educating one subgroup of students called Latinos of Mexican descent in ways that will be far more enriching for them and suitable for the United States. Therefore, we are asking today's educational leaders to be inventors and agents of change. To help practitioners reconstruct schools to educate Latino youths favorably, I have proposed ideas that run counter to the old ways. Some of the suggested ways can be put into practice within the existing structure, such as two-way communication (frequent, vertical, and horizontal), but when I propose moving away from the industrial model to a more holistic and naturalistic paradigm, it would be very helpful to shed as much of the legal restrictions as possible. Hence, whenever possible local school boards, superintendents, principals, and communities should consider utilizing the charter school status since charter schools are not held accountable for the same requirements as regular public schools. I offer this practical suggestion because it is well known that educators in conservative institutional roles prevent themselves from taking deviant action because of bureaucratic restrictions called policies.

Inventors do not limit themselves; they find ways to get around obstacles. This is one way to do so. Remember, as leaders we need to involve as many of the affected persons in the change process as possible so that they can help in thinking, planning, and actually bringing about the change. In so doing, change agents should remind themselves and others of the following:

1. The mission and purpose is to liberate everyone of old thinking and routine ways of acting.
2. Schools are systems where components are interrelated.
3. While schools are complex, they can be simplified.
4. Schools are people-dependent places where roles and relationships determine the interaction and outcomes.
5. Resources are important only from the standpoint of limiting or enhancing what you can do, not how much you can help students learn.
6. Education is a process where information is the tangible material, and critical thinking is the means to help individuals become independent and self-secure.

NOTES

1. In the 1990s, when Miami-Dade School District went from at-large elections to single-member representation, the board composition changed from having only one Hispanic member to five elected Latinos.

Part V

THE TRUMPETS HAVE SOUNDED

This book will help the reader move to the next stage, whatever that level may be. Some of you are becoming first-time believers, others are already believers, and still others have started the work of inventing welcoming places where human growth and other services are being offered to students, families, and communities. However, this book cannot be all things to all persons because readers are at different levels and may find themselves in different local circumstances. But having heard the trumpets, the *palomia* (a south Texas Spanish term used to connote a gathering of like minds) is growing. Chapter 9 is offered to help persons at different stages connect with other believers and learn from each other. Think of the last chapter of this book as the bridge that leads you to the next stage (whatever level that is) in your journey. Remember, the more difficult the road—and this will be a hard one—the stronger the traveler will become and ultimately the more enriching the experience.

Adelante (Onward)

Chapter Nine

A Call to Join the Action

After eight chapters, the reader should have a very good sense of what needs to be accomplished to transform schools so that they embrace the necessary building blocks: utilization of the Spanish language, incorporation of the Mexican and American cultures, development of full-service and community-centered facilities, thorough use of technology, use of data-driven instruction and decision making, and more. Some people and schools across the country have been at work transforming schools since the 1970s.[1] Others are just starting (1990s) and therefore are at different stages of their development. With this last chapter, two objectives will be accomplished: (1) to connect these island schools (works in progress) from north to south and from west to east and in so doing to create stronger and better schools and (2) to help practitioners in their efforts to advance the transformation of their schools by identifying links to more resources and technical assistance.

This book can only begin to bring the new Mexican American school into focus. Instead of the landscape photograph offered by this book, a set of blueprints is needed. But this book cannot develop such specifications because each community and each student body is different. Yes, there is commonality shared herein, a scaffold to help build anew. So to help both practitioner and academic bring about these new hothouses of learning, two types of general assistance are proposed. The first set of resources is listed within this chapter. It is divided into eight sections: I. Program Assistance; II. Community-Based Organizations; III. Schools to Watch and Learn From; IV. People; V. Funding Sources; VI. Publicly Elected Officials; VII. Books and Journals; and VIII. Multimedia Resources.

For those wanting to work on creating a lasting positive school that welcomes the entire community by providing not only instruction but also needed services, we encourage you to follow up with any and all of the resources listed.

However, one major strand throughout this book has been to discuss the dynamics of societal change. We know that people come and go (teachers move to other schools or districts, principals retire, superintendents go elsewhere). With the ever-increasing mobility in society, neighborhoods and their composition change as well. Also with the new economy, even the profile of cities is altered. In short, this resource list will be outdated soon after this book is published. So to keep up, stay current, and expand our way of learning, I propose capitalizing on our common-interest and ever-evolving technology. Modeling, if you will, a few concepts promoted herein, such as making contact with others of like interest, learning from each other, using homegrown data to help us make local decisions, and having technology work for us. How, you may ask.

The first step is developing a web page and list-serv to communicate with each other on a regular basis. The web page and list-serv will permit any one of us to ask questions, share approaches taken, and communicate any other matters of import. The second step is electronic. Put together an electronic newsletter, with the contents coming from practitioners, academics, graduate students, community leaders, and so on. Third, update and expand the list of resources provided in this chapter. In particular, add the names of schools and people, with descriptive information for each entry. Fourth, enlarge the resource sections to include conferences and book reviews, as well as list the latest instructional materials, software programs, films, and the like. Fifth, convene meetings, either national, regional, or state.

I am proposing that the Hispanic Border Leadership Institute (HBLI) at Arizona State University support the host server where the web page and list-serv are maintained; where the write-ups for the e-newsletter are collected and produced; where the resource list can be made current and expanded; and where we can coordinate national, regional, or state meetings. Of course this continued activity will happen only if there is sufficient interest expressed by the field. What do I mean? Not just casual inquiry (e.g., I need help, can you do this for me) but commitment to this transformation (i.e., we want to share and help each other in this mighty and much-needed labor). Let's develop a community of believers and doers, a national network of change agents dedicated to improving the education of children of color and the quality of living for brown communities. By so doing we can take pride in our achievements, knowing that we are creating welcoming places and schools where human growth is assured.

How will we know there is sufficient interest in peer-to-peer learning? After writing this book, I asked practitioners, school principals, college students, academics, community-based organization representatives, and others to express their interest in sharing technical assistance in order to form a strong network. Contact me at www.hbli.org or at Valverde@asu .edu if you wish to offer input.

RESOURCES

I. Program Assistance

After-School All-Stars
  9000 Sunset Blvd., Suite 1010
  Los Angeles, CA 90069
  Phone: (310) 275-3232
  Website: www.afterschoolallstars.org
  After-School All-Stars provides out-of-school programs that are fun for middle school kids, keep them safe, and help them achieve success in school and life. The program can be replicated anywhere across the country.

American Educational Research Association (AERA)
  1230 17th St. NW
  Washington, DC 20036
  Phone: (202) 223-9485
  Fax: (202) 775-1824
  Website: www.aera.net
  This association strives to improve the educational process by encouraging scholarly inquiry related to education.

Association of Mexican-American Educators (AMAE)
  P.O. Box 1673
  Freedom, CA 95019
  Phone: (909) 783-2069
  Website: www.amae.org

This association ensures equal access to a quality education at all levels for Mexican American/Latino students, where cultural and linguistic diversity is recognized and respected.

BUENO Center for Multicultural Education
University of Colorado
UCB 247, School of Education
Boulder, CO 80309-0249
Phone: (303) 492-5416
Website: www.colorado.edu/education/BUENO

The BUENO Center for Multicultural Education is an integral part of the School of Education at the University of Colorado at Boulder. Through a comprehensive range of research, training, and service projects, the center strongly promotes quality education with an emphasis on cultural pluralism. The center is deeply committed to facilitating equal educational support for cultural and language development.

California Latino Superintendents Association (CALSA)
19635 Redding Dr.
Salinas, CA 93908
Phone: (831) 455-8532
Website: www.calsa.org

CALSA is a professional association that brings together Latino educational leaders who are committed to quality public education.

California School Boards Association (CSBA)
3100 Beacon Blvd.
West Sacramento, CA 95691
Phone: (800) 266-3382
Website: www.csba.org

CSBA is a member-driven association that supports the governance team, school board members, superintendents, and senior administrative staff in its complex leadership role. It develops, communicates, and advocates the perspective of California school districts and county offices of education. Ask for Latino caucus contact information.

Chicano/Latino Policy Project (CLPP)
Institute for the Study of Social Change
University of California at Berkeley

2420 Bowditch St., Suite 5670
Berkeley, CA 94720-5670
Phone: (510) 642-6903
Fax: (510) 643-8844
Email: clppcuclink4@berkeley.edu
Website: www.clpr.berkeley.edu

CLPP is an affiliated research project of the Institute for the Study of Social Change at the University of California at Berkeley. CLPP's mission is to develop and support public policy research on domestic policy issues that affect the Latino community in the United States. CLPP promotes collaborative research; encourages and facilitates the exchange of ideas; provides research and training opportunities for faculty and for graduate and undergraduate students; disseminates policy-relevant publications; and conducts outreach meetings for the general public and elected officials.

The Civil Rights Project
  Harvard University
  125 Mt. Auburn St., 3rd floor
  Cambridge, MA 02138
  Phone: (617) 496-6367
  Fax: (617) 495-5210
  Website: www.civilrightsproject.harvard.edu

The mission of the Civil Rights Project is to renew the civil rights movement by bridging the worlds of ideas and action and by becoming a preeminent source of intellectual capital and a forum for building consensus within that movement.

The Education Trust
  1250 H St. NW, Suite 700
  Washington, D.C. 20005
  Phone: (202) 293-1217
  Website: www2.edtrust.org

The Education Trust works for the high academic achievement of all students at all levels, prekindergarten through college, and forever closing the achievement gaps that separate low-income students and students of color from other youth. The basic tenet is that all children will learn at high levels when they are taught at high levels.

Harvard Family Research Project
  Harvard University
  Graduate School of Education
  3 Garden Street
  Cambridge, MA
  Phone: (617) 495-9108
  Website: www.gse.harvard.edu/hfrp/projects/fine/resources/guide
  An online resource about what national organizations are doing in family involvement and homeschool partnerships. Specifically provides information on parent leadership development and collective engagement for school improvement and reform.

Hispanic Border Leadership Institute (HBLI)
  Arizona State University
  Main Campus
  P.O. Box 872411
  Tempe, AZ 85287-2411
  Phone: (480) 727-6364
  Fax: (480) 965-8497
  Website: www.hbli.org
  HBLI is dedicated to improving the education of Latinos, from prekindergarten to doctoral studies, by promoting systematic change via Latino leadership and policy development within the following groups: school board members; community college trustees; future executive officers of schools, colleges, state departments, and professional associations; and state legislators, congressional members, and civil leaders.

Intercultural Development Research Association (IDRA)
  5835 Callaghan Rd., Suite 350
  San Antonio, TX 78228-1190
  Phone: (210) 444-1710
  Fax: (210) 444-1714
  Email: contact@idra.org
  Website: www.idra.org
  IDRA conducts research and development activities; creates, implements, and administers innovative education programs; and provides teacher, administrator, and parent training and technical assistance.

Kids at Hope
  9040 W. Campbell Ave.
  Phoenix, AZ 85037
  Phone: (623) 772-2870
  Fax: (623) 877-8072
  Website: www.kidsathope.org

Through significant research and evaluation, Kids at Hope has developed a youth development strategy that begins with a belief system stating that all children are capable of success, with no exceptions; that is supported by a culture of individuals and organizations willing to suspend self-interest to accomplish a common good on behalf of all children; and finally that is enhanced by programs that permit and demonstrate how all children can succeed on their terms as well as our terms.

Mexican American Legal Defense and Educational Fund (MALDEF)
  National Parent/School Partnership Program
  634 S. Spring St.
  Los Angeles, CA 90014
  Phone: (213) 629-2512, ext. 120
  Fax: (213) 629-0266
  Website: www.maldef.org

MALDEF provides technical assistance and training for parents, teachers, and administrators in establishing parent leadership programs in their local districts; a national support network for Latino parents; a Latino parent involvement media awareness campaign; and an information advice line.

Mexican American School Board Members Association (MASBA)
  P.O. Box 160098
  San Antonio, TX 78280
  Phone: (210) 844-8698
  Fax: (210) 255-0041
  Email: MASBA@masba.net
  Website: www.masba.net

Headquartered in San Antonio, MASBA's mission is to help attain educational and cultural needs and opportunities in the public school system for Mexican American and other historically underserved or disadvantaged students. MASBA's activities comprise leadership development, public policy analysis, political awareness, parental education and involvement, and community empowerment.

National Association for Bilingual Education (NABE)
    1220 L St. NW, Suite 605
    Washington, DC 2005-4018
    Phone: (202) 898-1829
    Fax: (202) 789-2866
    Email: NABE@nabe.org
    Website: www.nabe.org
NABE publishes a newsletter, a journal, and policy papers regarding bilingual education. It holds a national conference each year.

National Council for Community and Education Partnerships (NCCEP)
    1400 20th St. NW, Suite G-1
    Washington, DC 20036
    Phone: (202) 530-1135
    Fax: (202) 530-0809
    Website: www.edpartnerships.org
NCCEP's guiding principles focus on expanding the educational opportunities of those students most often left behind.

National Clearinghouse for Bilingual Education (NCBE)
    George Washington University
    Graduate School of Education and Human Development
    2011 Eye St. NW, Suite 200
    Washington, DC 20006
    Phone: (202) 467-0867
    Fax: (800) 531-9347
    Website: www.ncela.gwu.edu
NCBE collects, analyzes, and disseminates information relating to the effective education of linguistically and culturally diverse learners in the United States through occasional publications, a regular email newsletter, and a comprehensive website with a searchable online database and full-text library.

National Council of La Raza
    1111 19th St. NW, Suite 1000
    Washington, DC 20036

Phone: (202) 785-1670
Fax: (202) 776-1794
Website: www.nclr.org
The council publishes reports and policy papers.

National Network of Partnership Schools
Johns Hopkins University
3003 N. Charles Street, Suite 200
Baltimore, MD 21218
Phone: (410) 516-8800
E-mail: nnps@csos.jhu.edu
Established by researchers at Johns Hopkins University, NNPS brings together schools, districts, and states that are committed to developing and maintaining comprehensive programs of school–family–community partnerships.

PALMS Project (Postsecondary Access for Latino Middle-Grades Students)
Educational Development Center, Inc. (EDC)
55 Chapel St.
Newton, MA 02458
Phone: (850) 683-8593
Fax: (617) 969-3440
Website: www.palmsproject.net
The PALMS Project, based at EDC, seeks to narrow the college knowledge gap so Latino parents can help their children attain a college education. The project features a website that provides up-to-date information and resources on college access programs and initiatives for middle school staff.

SchoolNet
525 7th Ave., 4th Floor
New York, NY 10018
Phone: (212) 645-0615
Website: www.schoolnet.com
SchoolNet works with leading school districts to implement instructional management solutions (IMS) to put data to work to assess performance, analyze trends, individualize instruction, and achieve results.

Southwest Center for Education Equity and Language Diversity at SEDL
   211 E. 7th St., Suite 200
   Austin, TX 78701-3253
   Phone: (512) 476-6861
   Toll free: (800) 476-6861
   Fax: (512) 476-2286
   Website: www.SEDL.org
SEDL is committed to long-term systemic, research, and experience-based solutions derived from research, development, evaluation, technical assistance, and professional development.

Tomás Rivera Policy Institute
   University of Southern California
   School of Policy, Planning, and Development
   Ralph and Goldie Lewis Hall
   650 Childs Way, Suite 102
   Los Angeles, CA 90089-0626
   Phone: (213) 821-5615
   Fax: (213) 821-1976
   Website: www.trpi.org
Founded in 1985, the Tomás Rivera Policy Institute advances critical, insightful thinking on key issues affecting Latino communities through objective, policy-relevant research, and its implications, for the betterment of the nation.

Transforming Schools for a Multicultural Society (TRANSFORMS)
   Patricia L. Guerra and Sarah W. Nelson
   8650 Spicewood Springs Rd., Suite 145-626
   Austin, TX 78759-4399
   Phone/Fax: 512-250-1880
   Website: www.transforms.biz
TRANSFORMS provides research-based staff development on culturally responsive learning environments. Its aim is to help educators develop beliefs and practices that lead to success for all students by taking participants on a journey of transformation through an intensive diversity training program. In this process, views of students and families are explored and reframed to allow educators to develop an equity lens.

WestEd
730 Harrison St.
San Francisco, CA 94107-1242
Phone: (415) 565-3000
Website: www.wested.org
Success for every learner is the goal of WestEd, a nonprofit research development and service agency. WestEd strives to enhance and increase education and human development within schools, families, and communities. Within the goal is one priority: serving underserved populations.

White House Initiative on Educational Excellence for Hispanic Americans
400 Maryland Ave. SW
Washington, DC 20202
Phone: (202) 401-1411
Fax: (202) 401-8377
Website: www.yic.gov
This group has sponsored reports on Hispanic education.

II. Community-Based Organizations

Cesar E. Chavez Foundation
500 N Brand Blvd., Suite 1650
Glendale, CA 91203
Phone: (818) 265-0300
Website: www.chavezfoundation.org
The mission of the foundation is to maximize human potential to improve communities by preserving, promoting, and applying the legacy and universal values of civil rights leader Cesar E. Chavez. Check the website for information on regional offices.

Chicanos Por La Causa (CPLC)
1112 E Buckeye Rd.
Phoenix, AZ 85034-4043
Phone: (602) 257-0700
Fax: (602) 256-2740
Website: www.cplc.org
CPLC is committed to building stronger, healthier communities by being a leading advocate, coalition builder, and direct service provider.

CPLC promotes sufficiency to enhance the quality of life for the benefit of those it serves.

Friendly House, Inc.
    802 S. First Ave.
    Phoenix, AZ 85003
    Phone: (602) 257-1870
    Fax: (602) 254-3135
    Website: www.friendlyhouse.org
The Friendly House mission is to foster excellence in the community by serving the educational and human service needs of its people. Its emphasis is on the education of its youth, employment and training, social services, and adult education.

Logan Square Neighborhood Association (LSNA)
    2840 N. Milwaukee Ave.
    Chicago, IL 60618
    Phone: (773) 384-4370
    Fax: (773) 384-0624
    Website: www.lsna.net
One objective of LSNA is to open schools to communities. Started in 1993, LSNA has transformed eight schools into community-based facilities, has changed the way schools and families interact with one another, and is now a national model for an effective approach to involving parents in school reform. Logan Square is a mixed-income Chicago community of about 85,000 people, two-thirds of whom are Latino. More than 50% drop out of the schools, which are too large and have too few resources.

TELACU (The East Los Angeles Community Union)
    5400 E. Olympic Blvd.
    Los Angeles, CA 90022
    Phone: (213) 721-1655
    Fax: (213) 724-3372
    Website: www.telacu.com
TELACU is a nonprofit community development corporation committed to service, empowerment, advancement, and the creation of self-sufficiency by providing the tools to rebuild and enhance the communities it serves.

III. Schools to Watch and Learn From

Camino Nuevo Charter Academy
697 S. Burlington Ave.
Los Angeles, CA 90057
Phone: (213) 413-4245
Website: www.caminonuevo.org

Carl Hayden Community High School
3333 W. Roosevelt St.
Phoenix, AZ 85009
Contact: Steve Ybarra, principal
Phone: (602) 764-3000
Website: www.hayden.edu

Cesar E. Chavez High School
3921 W. Baseline Rd.
Laveen, AZ 85339
Contact: Dr. James McElroy, principal
Phone: (602) 764-4005
Website: www.cesarchavezhighschool.org

Coral Way Elementary School
Miami-Dade County Public Schools
1950 SW 13th Ave.
Miami, FL 33145
Phone: (305) 854-0515
Website: coralwayelementary.dadeschools.net/index2.html

Edcouch-Elsa High School
Edcouch-Elsa Independent School District
N Yellowjacket Dr.
Elsa, TX 78543
Phone: (956) 262-6074
Website: http://highschool.eeisd.org/
For more information about Edcouch-Elsa High School, see the June 2005 issue of *Principal Leadership* (pp. 16–21), printed by the National Association of Secondary School Principals.

Logan Square Neighborhood Schools (Chicago, IL)

Ames Elementary	Goethe Elementary
Chase Elementary	Monroe Elementary
Chicago International Charter, Bucktown	Mozart Elementary
Darwin Elementary	Pulaski Academy
Drummond Elementary	Yates Elementary
Funston Elementary	

See the Logan Square website (www.lsna.net) for more information about these schools.

Strawberry Mansion High School
3133 Ridge Ave.
Philadelphia, PA 19132
Contact: Lois Powell-Mondesire, principal
Phone: (215) 684-5089
Website: www.phila.k12.pa.us/offices/psit/schools/strawberry.html
Strawberry Mansion is an alternative school in Denver, CO.

IV. People

Dr. John Barcey, superintendent
Scottsdale Unified School District
Education Center
3811 N. 44th St.
Phoenix, AZ 85018-5420
Phone: (480) 484-6120
Fax: (480) 484-6293
Website: www.susd.org

Sal Castro, retired
Los Angeles Unified School District
Director, Chicano Youth Leadership Conference, Inc.
Los Angeles, CA
Email: cylcincla@yahoo.com

Dr. Rosie Castro Feinberg, retired
Former school board member, Miami-Dade Public School
Director of Bilingual Technical Assistance Center, University of Miami

Miami, FL
Email: rcastro@fiu.edu

Dr. Kino Flores, superintendent
Tolleson Union High School District
9419 W Van Buren St.
Tolleson, AZ 85353
Phone: (623) 478-4000
Fax: (623) 478-4196
Website: www.tuhsd.org

Dr. Jose Leyba
Provost of Downtown Campus
Maricopa Community College District
2411 W. 14th St.
Tempe, AZ 85281
Phone: (480) 731-8930
Former principal and superintendent in the greater Phoenix city area.

Jeff MacSwan, associate professor
Curriculum and Instruction
Arizona State University
College of Education
Email: jeff.macswan@asu.edu
Expert in language instruction for English language learners (ELLs).

Dr. William "Bill" Rojas, retired
Superintendent in New York, San Francisco, and Dallas
Email: wrojas@ad.com

Dr. Angela Valenzuela, associate professor
Education and Mexican American Studies
University of Texas at Austin
Austin, TX
Email: valenz@mail.utexas.edu

V. Funding Sources

Bill and Melinda Gates Foundation
  P.O. Box 23350
  Seattle, WA 98102
  Phone: (206) 709-3100
  Website: www.gatesfoundation.org
  Education Program
  Phone: (206) 709-3607
  Email: edinfo@gatesfoundation.org
  Grant Inquiries
  Phone: (206) 709-3140
  Email: info@gatesfoundation.org

The foundation's education program aims to increase the number of students, particularly low-income African Americans and Hispanics, who graduate with the high-level skills they need for success in college and at work. The foundation's education initiative is a collaborative effort to improve education at the school, district, and state levels, and its scholarship programs are focused on reducing the financial obstacles that keep qualified minority students from entering and continuing college.

W.K. Kellogg Foundation
  1 Michigan Ave. E
  Battle Creek, MI 49017-4012
  Phone: (269) 968-1611
  Website: www.wkkf.org

Grants are distributed in four areas: health, food systems and rural development, youth and education, and philanthropy and volunteerism.

National Endowment for the Humanities
  1100 Pennsylvania Ave. NW
  Washington, DC 20506
  Phone: (800) NEH-1121
  Website: www.neh.gov

NEH serves and strengthens our Republic by promoting excellence in humanities and conveying the lessons of history to all Americans. It accomplishes this mission by providing grants in four funding areas: preserving and providing access to cultural resources, education, research, and public programs.

State Farm Companies Foundation
   Youth Service America
   1101 15th St., Suite 200
   Washington DC, 20005
   Phone: (202) 296-2992
   Website: www.ysa.org
State Farm Good Neighbor Service Learning grants enable youths and educators to bring the positive benefits of service learning to more young people across America.

Tiger Woods Foundation
   4281 Katella Ave., Suite 111
   Los Alamitos, CA 90720
   Phone: (714) 816-1806
   Website: www.twfound.org
Tiger Woods Foundation grants focus on providing opportunities to children who are underserved, focusing on programs and projects that enhance the learning process for children and transitional programs for young adults to become productive adults.

VI. Publicly Elected Officials

Honorable Ruben Hinojosa
   U.S. Representative, South Texas
   DC address:
   The Honorable Ruben Hinojosa
   United States House of Representatives
   3463 Rayburn House Office Building
   Washington, DC 20515-4315
   Phone: (202) 225-2531
   Fax: (202) 225-5688
   Website: www.house.gov/hinojosa
   District office:
   107 S St. Mary's St.
   Beeville, TX 78102
   Phone: (361) 358-8400
   Fax: (361) 358-8407

Honorable Ed Pastor
U.S. Congressman, 4th District of Arizona
DC address:
The Honorable Ed Pastor
United States House of Representatives
2465 Rayburn House Office Building
Washington, DC 20515-0304
Phone: (202) 225-4065
Fax: (202) 225-1655
Website: www.house.gov/pastor
District office:
411 N Central Ave., Suite 150
Phoenix, AZ 85004
Phone: (602) 256-0551

National Association of Latino Elected and Appointed Officials (NALEO)
Educational Fund
1122 W. Washington Blvd., 3rd Floor
Los Angeles, CA 90015
Phone: (213) 747-7606
Email: info@naleo.org
Website: www.naleo.org
NALEO develops and implements programs that promote the integration of Latino immigrants into American society, develops future leaders among Latino youths, provides assistance and training to the nation's Latino elected and appointed officials, and conducts research on issues important to the Latino population.

VII. Books and Journals

Calderon, Margarita E., & Minaya-Rowe, Liliana. (2003). *Designing and Implementing Two-Way Bilingual Programs.* Thousand Oaks, CA: Corwin.
Castro-Feinberg, Rosie. (2002). *Bilingual Education: A Reference Handbook.* Santa Barbara: ABC-Clio.
Cummins, Jim. (1996). *Negotiating Identities: Educating for Empowerment in a Diverse Society.* Covina: California Association of Bilingual Education.

Delpit, Lisa. (1995). *Other People's Children: Cultural Conflict in the Classroom.* New York: New Press.

Gaitan, Concha D. (2004). *Involving Latino Families in Schools.* Thousand Oaks, CA: Corwin.

Levine, David (Ed.). (1995). *Rethinking Schools: An Agenda for Change.* New York: New Press.

Michie, Gregory. (2004). *See You When We Get There: Teachin,* for *Change in Urban Schools.* New York: Teachers College Press.

Nieto, Sonia. (1999). *The Light in Their Eyes: Creating Multicultural Learning Communities.* New York: Teachers College Press.

Noguera, Pedro. (2003). *City Schools and the American Dream.* New York: Teachers College Press.

Schneidewind, Nancy, & Davidson, Ellen. (1998). *Open Minds to Equality: A Sourcebook of Learning Activities to Affirm Diversity and Promote Equity.* Boston: Allyn & Bacon.

Senge, Peter M., Cambron-McCabe, Nelda, Lucas, Timothy, Smith, Bryan, Dutton, Janis, & Kleiner, Art. (2005). *Schools that Learn.* New York: Random House.

Sentilles, Sarah. (2005). *Taught by America: A Story of Struggle and Hope in Compton.* Boston: Beacon.

VIII. Multimedia Resources

The Journal: Technological Horizons in Education, published monthly by 101 Communications LLC, 9121 Oakdale Ave., Suite 101, Chatsworth, CA 91311. See www.thejournal.com.

The Problem We All Live With: Inequalities between Boston's Urban and Suburban Schools, DVD (2004). Available through Teaching for Change, Washington, DC.

Public Education Network (PEN@PublicEducation.org)
Online NewsBlast provided on a weekly basis, typically Fridays, gives summary coverage of education matters and listings of current grants available for application by schools.

Reinventing Education Change Toolkit (www.reinventingeducation.org)
The Reinventing Education Change Toolkit is a website created by IBM to help education professionals be more effective at leading and implementing change. It was created through the collaborative effort of

Rosabeth Moss Kanter and Goodmeasure, Inc., IBM's Reinventing Education project, together with the Council of Chief State School Officers, National Association of Secondary School Principals, and National Association of Elementary School Principals. The site provides online access to proven frameworks for leading and managing change; diagnostic tools for assessment; and collaborative tools, including interactive worksheets, planning tools, and an online discussion area.

CONCLUSION

The trumpets have sounded, in some places louder than others. The call to join in remaking schools better, more hospitable, more effective learning places has been placed. Join with those who have pledged and started work to create new schools that will ensure every single one of our Latino students is connected to and engaged in their learning, where families are welcomed and involved honestly in the educational process. These new schools are truly part of the larger communities they serve, drawing in other agencies as resources to complement and enhance the human development of the whole student.

NOTES

1. As early as 1976, Crystal City, Texas, started to convert its schools with assistance from a Rockefeller Foundation Grant. Jose Angel Gutierrez, then leader of the Raza Unida political party, realized that schools had to be reflections of the communities they served and that Chicano students could not walk from home to enter a foreign place called school.

Glossary

Following are initials and terms used by educators as quick references and ways to identify common professional organizations and educational programs. They are provided in alphabetical order.

AERA	American Educational Research Association
AFT	American Federation of Teachers
ASCD	Association for Supervision and Curriculum Development
Dual-language school	Two languages are used for instruction with all students in the school; one language is English.
ELL	English language learner
ESEA	Elementary and Secondary Education Act
ESL	English as a second language
LEP	Limited English proficient
Maintenance	Language instruction of the student's home language is used throughout the student's school years.
NABE	National Association for Bilingual Education
NASB	National Association of School Boards
NASSP	National Association of Secondary School Principals
NCLB	No Child Left Behind
NEA	National Education Association
Title I	Compensatory educational programs offered by the federal government under the ESEA.

Title VII	Bilingual and bicultural educational programs offered by the federal government under the ESEA.
Transitional	The student's native language is used until he or she is able to learn in English.
Two-way	Two languages are used to instruct all students in the school; however, teachers rotate into classrooms.

References

Alliance for Excellent Education. (2005). *Straight A's: Public Education Policy and Progress, 5*(6).

Alonzo-Dunsmoor, Monica. (2005, March 16). Mexican Consul Offers Boost to Parents, Kids: Official Visits "Failing" School. *Arizona Republic,* p. B5.

Andersson, Theodore, & Boyer, Mildred. (1970). *Bilingual Schooling in the United States* (Vols. 1–2). Austin: University of Texas Press.

Arens, S. A. (2005). *Examining the Meaning of Accountability: Reframing the Construct.* Aurora, CO: Mid-continent Research for Education and Learning (McREL).

August, D., & Hakuta, K. (1998). *Improving Schooling for Language-Minority Children: Research Agenda.* Washington, DC: National Academy Press.

Banks, James (Ed.). (1989). *Multicultural Education: Issues and Perspectives.* Boston: Allyn & Bacon.

Bolman, Lee G., & Deal, Terrance E. (2001). *Leading with Soul: An Uncommon Journey of Spirit.* Hoboken, NJ: Wiley.

Brown v. Topeka, Kansas. (1954). United States Supreme Court 347 US 483 (USSC+).

Burger, Edward B., & Starbird, Michael. (2005). *Coincidences, Chaos, and All that Math Jazz: Making Light of Weighty Ideas.* NY: Norton.

Cardenas, Jose A., & Cardenas, Bambalina. (1972). The Theory of Cultural Incompatibility. Unpublished paper, San Antonio, Texas.

Carter, Thomas P. (1970). *Mexican Americans in Schools: A History of Educational Neglect.* New York: College Entrance Examination Board.

Center on Education Policy. (2005). *Do You Know the Latest Good News about American Education?* Washington, DC: CEP.

Chapa, Jorge, & De La Rosa, Belinda. (2004). Latino Population Growth: Socioeconomic and Demographic Characteristics and Implications for Educational Attainment. *Education and Urban Society Journal, 36*(2), 130–149.

Chronicle of Higher Education. (2001, August 31). *Almanac* (Vol. XLVIII), no. 1.

Cisneros v. Corpus Christi Independent School District, Civil Action No. 68-C-95 (Southern District of Texas, June 1970).

Clavell, James (producer and director). (1967). *To Sir, with Love* [Film]. Columbia Studios.

Clinton, Bill. (2005, October 28). Speech at the Texas Book Festival, Austin, Texas.

Collier, Virginia. (1987). Age and Rate of Acquisition of Second Language for Academic Purposes. *TESOL Quarterly, 21*(4), 617–641.

Combs, Arthur W. (1962). *Perceiving, Behaving, and Becoming: A New Arthur W. Combs Focus for Education.* Alexandria, VA: Association of Supervision and Curriculum Development.

Covey, Stephen. (1989). *The Seven Habits of Highly Effective People: Restoring the Character Ethic.* New York: Simon & Schuster.

Cummings, James. (1981). Age on Arrival and Immigrant Second-Language Learning in Canada: A Reassessment. *Applied Linguistics, 11*(2), 132–149.

Darby, Robert, & Hughes, Tim. (2005). The Evolution of Student Information Systems. *T.H.E. Journal, 33*(3), 38.

Doyle, Denis P. (2005). Peter Drucker, Thanks for the Memories. *The Doyle Report, 5.46*(135) (Reported in SchoolNet Publication).

Duran, Richard P. (1983). *Hispanics' Education and Background.* New York: College Entrance Examination Board.

Education Commission of the States. (2005). *Prisoners of Time.* Reprint of the 1994 report of the National Commission on Time and Learning. Denver, CO: ECS.

Eisner, Elliot. (1985). *The Art of Educational Evaluation.* London: Falmer.

Eisner, Elliot. (2002). *The Arts and the Creation of Mind.* New Haven: Yale University Press.

Fairlie, Robert. (2005, October). Are We Really a Nation On-Line? Ethnic and Racial Disparities in Access to Technology and Their Consequences. Paper presented at the Leadership Conference, Washington, DC.

Foreman, Carl (producer), & Thompson, J. Lee (director). (1961). *The Guns of Navarone* [Film]. Columbia Studios.

Friedman, J. (2005, September 26) Investment Firms Focusing on Latinos' Purchasing Power. *L.A. Times*, p. C1, C6.

Garcia, Shernaz, & Guerra, Patricia. (2003). Do We Truly Believe All Children Can Learn? Implications for Comprehensive School Reform. *Adelante Newsletter, 4*(1), 5.

Gee, Paul James. (2003). *What Video Games Have to Teach Us about Learning and Literacy.* New York: Palgrave/Macmillan.

Gehrke, Robert. (2003, August 30). New Navajo School Culturally Sensitive. *Arizona Republic,* p. A35.

Gibson, William, & Rodriguez, Ibosvani. (2005, October 17). Migrant Workers on Gulf Coast Face Exploitation. *Boston Globe,* p. A3.

Gutek, Gerald L. (Ed). (2004). *A Historical Introduction to American Education* (2nd ed.). Long Grove, IL: Waveland.

Hess, F. (2002). *School Board at the Turn of the 21st Century.* Washington, DC: National School Board Association.

Hines, Larry. (2005). Interactive Learning Environment Keeps Modesto Students Engaged. *T.H.E. Journal, 33*(2), 40.

Hodgekinson, Harold. (1999). *All One System: A Second Look.* Washington, DC: Institute of Educational Leadership.

Horowitz, Jordan. (2005). *Inside Higher School Reform: Making the Changes that Matter.* San Francisco: WestEd.

Intercultural Development Research Association. (2001, September). *Newsletter XXVII*(9), 10.

Kantor, Rosabeth M. (2005, October). From "Resistance Is Everywhere" to "Resistance Is Futile": Helpful Hints for Leading Change. *Education Leadership Newsletter* [Online]. Available: www.reinventingeducation.org/RE3Web/ newsletters.

Kendall, Diana (Ed.). (1997). *Race, Class, and Gender in a Diverse Society.* Boston: Allyn & Bacon.

Kennedy, John F. (1961, January 9). Message to the Massachusetts Legislature, Cambridge.

Key Data: Hispanic Clout. (2004, November 22). Knight Ridder/Tribune Information Services [Online]. Available: www.krtdirect.com.

Kindler, A. (2002). *Survey of the States' Limited English Proficient Students and Available Educational Programs, 2000–2001, Summary Report.* Washington, DC: National Clearinghouse for English Language Acquisition and Language Instruction Educational Programs.

Lawrence-Lightfoot, S. (1978). *Worlds Apart: Relationships Between Families and Schools.* NY: Basic.

Los Angeles Unified School District. (2004–2005). Fact Sheet [Online]. Available: www.lausd.k12.ca.us.

MacSwan, Jeff. (2005). How Long Does It Take Immigrant Students to Learn English? *Show and Tell* (Fall), 26–29.

Mollin, Gaetana. (2005). Hoover Elementary Turns to LeapFrog SchoolHouse. *T.H.E. Journal, 33*(2), 48.

National Assessment of Educational Progress (NAEP). (2005). *National Report Card.* Washington, D.C.: U.S. Department of Education.

National Association of Secondary School Principals. (1996). *Breaking Ranks: Changing an American Institution.* Reston, VA: NASSP.

National Association of Secondary School Principals. (2005). *Creating a Culture of Literacy: A Guide for Middle and High School Principals.* Reston, VA: NASSP.

National Center for Educational Statistics. (2003). *Characteristics of Public Schools, Annual Reports* [Online]. Available: www.nces.ed.gov/.

National Center for Education Statistics. (2005). Elementary and Secondary Enrollments [Online]. Available: www.nces.ed.gov/pubs2005.

National Network of Partnership Schools (NNPS). (2005). *Promising Partnership Practices 2005.* Baltimore: Johns Hopkins University.

National School Board Association. (2005a). E-Rate Bill Seeks to Avoid Funding Disruption. *School Board News, 25*(13), 1.

National School Board Association. (2005b). NCLB Lawsuits Highlight Problems about How the Law Is Working. *School Board News, 25*(13), 5.

New Leaders for New Schools (NLNS). (2005). Five Core Beliefs [Online]. Available: www.nlns.org.

Nichols, Sharon L., & Berliner, David. (March 2005). *The Inevitable Corruption of Indicators and Education through High-Stakes Testing.* Tempe, AZ: ASU Education Public Policy Laboratory.

Orfield, Gary, & Eaton, Susan. (1996). *The Dismantling Desegregation: The Quiet Reversal of* Brown v. Board of Education. New York: Free Press.

Palmer, Lisa. (2005, October 16). Mathematics Made Fun. *Boston Globe,* p. B9.

Peters, Thomas, & Waterman, Robert H. (1982). *In Search of Excellence: Lessons from America's Best Run Companies.* New York: Harper.

Peterson, Bob. (1995). Which Side Are You On? In David Levine, Robert Lowe, Bob Peterson, & Rita Tenorio (Eds.), *Rethinking Schools* (pp. 253–263). New York: New Press.

Plessy v. Ferguson (United States Supreme Court, 1896). 163 US 537.

Podoll, Sue, & Randle, Darcy. (2005). Building a Virtual High School . . . Click by Click. *T.H.E. Journal, 33*(2), 15–19.

Public Law 94-142. (1975, November 29). Education for All Handicapped Children Act of 1975 [Online]. Available: http://asclepius.com/angel/special.html.

Ramirez, Manuel, & Castaneda, Alfredo. (1974). *Cultural Democracy, Bicognitive Development, and Education.* New York: Academic.

Rosenthal, Robert, & Jacobson, Lenore. (1992). *Pygmalion in the Classroom: Teacher Expectation and Pupils' Intellectual Development.* Norwalk, CT: Crown House.

Ryman, Anne, & Madrid, Ofelia. (2004, January 17). Hispanics Upset by Teacher's Discipline. *Arizona Republic,* p. B1.

Sanchez, George I. (Ed.). (1946). *First Regional Conference on the Education of Spanish-Speaking People in the Southwest.* Education Occasional Papers, No. 1. Austin: University of Texas Press.

Sarason, Seymour B. (1990). *The Predictable Failure of Educational Reform.* San Francisco: Jossey-Bass.

Senge, Peter. (2005). *Schools that Learn.* New York: Doubleday.

Senge, Peter M. (1994). *The Fifth Discipline: The Art and Practice of the Learning Organization* (2nd ed.). New York: Doubleday.

Shapiro, Joan, & Stefkovich, Jacqueline. (2005). *Ethical Leadership and Decision Making in Education.* Mahwah, NJ: Erlbaum.

Spring, Joel H. (1976). *The Sorting Machine: National Education Policy Since 1945.* New York: McKay.

Staton, Ron. (2005, March 12). Revival of Hawaiian Language. *Arizona Republic,* p. A37.

Suro, Roberto. (1998). *Strangers among Us: How Latino Immigration Is Transforming America.* New York: Knopf.

Teachers: Giving Back to Alma Mater. (2004, February 5). *Arizona Republic,* p. B1.

Texas School Finance Decision. (2004, September 16). *Arizona Republic*, p. A5.

Tuttle, Kate. (2005). What's Wrong with a Six-Hour School Day. *Ed. The Magazine of the Harvard Graduate School of Education* (Summer), 20.

Tyack, David B. (1974). *One Best System: A History of American Urban Education.* Cambridge, MA: Harvard University Press.

U.S. Census Bureau. (2000). FactFinder [Online]. Available: www.census.gov/main/access.html.

U.S. Census Bureau. (2002). *Current Population Survey.* Ethnic and Hispanic Statistics Branch. Washington, DC: USCB.

U.S. Census Bureau. (2003). Statistical Data Release [Online]. Available: www.census.gov/main/access.html.

U.S. Census Bureau. (2005). U.S. Census 2005 Count [Online]. Available: www.census.gov/main/access.html.

U.S. Commission on Civil Rights. (1970–1976). *A Series of 8 Reports on the Education of Mexican Americans in the Southwest.* Washington, DC: U.S. Government Printing Office.

U.S. Department of Education. (1983). *A Nation at Risk.* Washington, DC: USDE.

Valverde, L. A., & Scribner, K. (2001). Latino Students: Organizing for Greater Achievement. *NASSP Bulletin, 85*(624), 22–31.

Valverde, Leonard A. (Ed.). (2002). *A Compromised Commitment.* Tempe, AZ: Hispanic Border Leadership Institute.

Voisin, D. R., Salazar, L. F., Crosby, R., Diclemente, R. J., Yarber, W. L., & Staples-Horn, M. (2005). Teacher Connectedness and Health-Related Outcomes among Detained Adolescents. *Journal of Adolescent Health, 37*(4), 337.

Warren, Mark R. (2005). Communities and Schools: A New View of Urban Education Reform. *Harvard Education Review, 75*(2), 133–160.

Weick, K. (1976). Educational Organizations as Loosely Compiled Systems. *EAQ, 21*, 1–19.

White House Initiative on Educational Excellence for Hispanic Americans. (2002). *From Risk to Opportunity: Fulfilling the Educational Needs of Hispanic Americans in the 21st Century.* Washington, DC: White House.

Wingett, Yvonne. (2005, October 11). 2nd-Generation Latinos Mean Wave of Change. *Arizona Republic,* p. A1.

Index